Infallible proofs

MARVIN BYERS

ISBN 978-1-7325440-7-9

For Worldwide Distribution

Printed in the United States of America

Cover design: Daniela Uriarte

A Publication of

HEBRON PRESS

Hebron Ministries, Inc.

Inside the U.S. you may call, toll-free, to order this book at:

1-800-**LAST DAY** (1-800-527-8329) or

(502) 2333-2615 in Guatemala City, Central America

You can also reach us through the Internet at:
www.hebronministries.com

TABLE OF CONTENTS

ACKNOWLEDGMENTS

Many of the experiences that I write about in this book were great blessings, but some of them also involved great trials.

In both trials and blessings, my loving wife, Barbara, has faithfully walked with me throughout all of our journey during these many years. She has often been a great encouragement to me, and has carried a greater burden than I have, and she surely deserves a greater reward.

I would also like to express my deep appreciation to Pastor David Machado. Although he is extremely busy, he was willing to edit this book. I have learned by experience that he is one of the most capable editors that I know.

CHAPTER 1

Infallible Proofs for Honest Hearts

After the Lord's resurrection, "He shewed himself alive after his passion by many infallible proofs" (Acts 1:3). The disciples urgently needed Him to do so. They were under enormous emotional and spiritual pressures, attacks, and doubts. The Lord knew that after His ascension to heaven even greater doubts would assail them unless He gave them indisputable proofs that He was alive and real. If He had merely appeared to them on various occasions after His resurrection and then ascended, Satan would have had a field day with them by planting serious doubts in their hearts. Can't you hear Satan speaking through one or more of them later on?

Maybe doubting Thomas would have said, "Brethren, when we gathered in the upper room several days after the cross, we thought that Jesus appeared to us there. But have any of you realized that the extent of our grief for His death was so great that we probably allowed our imaginations to run wild? What we saw was probably nothing more than a figment of our imagination, the fruit of our grieving souls. What really happened was that when the first person declared he was seeing Him, we all began to see Him through the eyes of our broken hearts."

We know that Thomas did, in fact, express related doubts after His appearance to the others in the upper room. Thomas wasn't present during one of His first appearances, and the other ten could not convince him that they had seen anything more than a vision (John 20:24–28). Since he obviously wasn't calling them liars, he must have concluded that they had seen nothing more than a vision of some sort, not their actual Lord.

Infallible proofs erased all possible doubts. On one occasion, while He was with them in the upper room, He asked them if they had anything to eat. They gave Him fish and a honeycomb, and He took and ate them in their presence (Luke 24:41–43). Can you just imagine what might have happened after He departed on that occasion? Someone could have said, "Brethren, do you think that the Lord was literally with us a few moments ago, or were we all merely seeing a vision?" At that point, the others could have exclaimed, "Wait a minute! Moments ago, we had fish and a honeycomb here on the table. You all saw Him eat them. They are no longer in this room! He was truly with us in His resurrected body!" This was most certainly a very small infallible proof that He gave them, compared to others. Nonetheless, it left absolutely no doubt in their hearts that they had seen the Lord.

As His disciples today, at least some of us would admit that there are moments when we feel the onslaughts of the wicked one who attacks us by planting doubts in our hearts. Even Jesus experienced such an attack when Satan came to Him and sought to plant doubts in His heart about what the Father had audibly spoken at His baptism. The Father's voice from heaven declared, "This is My Beloved Son" (Matthew 3:17), and the Devil came and said, "If You are the Son of God . . ." (Matthew 4:3).

Are we to assume that the men who walked with the Lord for several years needed more proof of His resurrection than we need today? Do we need infallible proofs of the reality of Jesus or is that no longer necessary because we are such giants of faith? Or, are we to conclude that the Lord showed those disciples favors that He is not willing to show us today? If such be the case, then either He has changed the way He deals with man, or else He shows respect of persons. The Bible tells us that He never changes, and that *He is the same yesterday, and today, and forever* (Hebrews 13:8), and that He is no respecter of persons (Acts 10:34).

Could it be that the Lord still gives to man infallible proofs of His resurrection and of His existence? Maybe He continues to give them, but we ignore them, or we are so blinded that we don't even notice them. I want to share some of the infallible proofs of the reality of our Savior that my wife and I have personally experienced, along with the experiences of others whom we have personally known. All of these experiences are verifiable through many witnesses, as well as documents.

I realize that "The fool hath said in his heart, there is no God" (Psalm 14:1). I also realize there will be some who will read the events that are recorded in the following pages and they will still conclude that there is no God. Some people are determined to be fools until their dying day. Solomon referred to them when he wrote, "Though thou shouldest bray a fool in a mortar among wheat with a pestle, yet will not his foolishness depart from him" (Proverbs 27:22). Some people simply love being fools, and no matter what God does or what happens to them, they will remain fools. They are unwilling to acknowledge the existence of God because of the personal implications it would entail, like knowing that they are answerable for the way they live. That knowledge might give them sleep apnea! They prefer being sedated by ignorance.

The source of their ignorance is revealed by the apostle Peter: "For this they *willingly are ignorant* of, that by the word of God the heavens were of old . . ." (2 Peter 3:5). They actually *want* to be ignorant. For them, ignorance is bliss for now, but its cost will be eternal damnation.

Some who are fools will dismiss every experience in this book as nothing more than coincidences. However, anyone who honestly considers these experiences will be faced with a simple fact. In any given experience so many coincidences had to have occurred to bring about the outcome, that only God could have brought them all together. Of course, the fools who reject God also happily embrace the ignorance that declares that if the temperature is right, and it is given enough time to arrange itself, a thin soup in the ocean will turn into human beings. This is the bottom line in the wild speculation referred to as evolution.

The Creation Itself is the Greatest Proof

The creation itself is the greatest infallible proof of God's existence. Referring to God, Romans 1:20 declares, "For the invisible things of him from the creation of the world are clearly seen, being understood by the things that are made, even his eternal power and Godhead; so that they are without excuse."

The discovery of DNA has, in numerous ways, decidedly put to rest the myth that the first living cell came about by some accidental or sublime event of nature, as the evolutionists claim happened. DNA consists of two very long and complex molecules with an enormous amount of information encoded into them. The two long molecules are intertwined to form a double helix. One of them has been referred to as a mirror image of the other. Scientists recognize that DNA is a major secret to life itself. But to form the first simple living cell, the two molecules had to "accidentally" form in precisely the same place in a vast ocean and at precisely the same time. Coincidentally, one had to be the mirror image of the other, and they then had to somehow get intimately intertwined.

At this point, the problem for an evolutionist has hardly begun, because approximately 200 other substances are needed for a simple cell to reproduce itself. The evolutionists must believe that they all formed at the same time and place in which the double helix formed in a vast ocean. The epitome of the absurd is that they also must believe that the enormously complex cell wall had to somehow form at the same time and place, through a miracle of nature, and then the cell wall accidentally enclosed the double helix and the 200 substances all at once! Believing this requires an almost infinite "faith," and a willing ignorance of a simple reality—the improbability of all this happening is definitely infinite. It is far easier to lift our faith heavenward, and recognize that only a powerful Creator could have created life.

Also, the concept of evolution is in total violation of the second law of thermodynamics that Robert Clausius discovered in 1850. That law essentially states that every system in the Universe, left to itself, goes from order to disorder. For example, any building left to itself will decay and be in ruins in time. A clock will run down and stop working. Without God, the solar system itself will cease to exist once the sun's limited amount of energy is expended. Maybe without realizing it, every evolutionist has chosen to believe in the myth of evolution that defies an inviolable law of physics. For those who have delved into the subject, they will recognize that the following statement is true: The bottom line of the hypothesis of evolution[1] is that hydrogen gas given enough time can convert itself into human beings and all the rest of God's awesome creation.[2]

---

1   The name that scientists themselves gave to the myth of evolution is "The Theory of Evolution." According to modern science, ideas develop through three progressive stages: 1) hypothesis, 2) theory, and 3) law. True science cannot call evolution a theory, an idea supported by evidence. Rather, it is merely a hypothesis, an unproven idea. I had three majors in the University of Michigan: chemistry, physics, and math. For those who are interested, I give a study on evolution from a scientist's point of view, and show scientifically that, far from having supporting evidence, science in the last 30 years has proven beyond any doubt that evolution never happened. However, in every generation, the great minds of the world have believed one or more myths as fact, and we have not escaped that plague today. Furthermore, men are almost always unwilling to forsake their favorite myth. To obtain a copy of the study on evolution that I have given in both English and Spanish, go to www.hebronministries.com.

2   According to the Big Bang concept, the only thing that initially existed in the Universe was hydrogen gas, the most basic and only element after the Big Bang.

What Crawled Out of the Waters First?

According to the theory of evolution, over time, the first simple cell turned into fish. Then, with the passing of millions of years, some fish developed legs and lungs, and they crawled out of the water to live as fish-frogs. I have never heard any evolutionist explain what the first fish-frog ate. Did the insects crawl out of the water millions of years before the first fish-frog crawled out? Did the plants crawl out of the water millions of years before? They, too, consist of living cells. Also, are we to assume that when the first fish-frog crawled out, that actually two crawled out together—a male and a female fish-frog? Otherwise, there would have been no procreation, and with the death of the first fish-frog, the entire process would have had to begin again.

I am thankful that the Creator brought incredible order to this world, including giving us bodies so complex that humanity is still far from fully understanding them. He intervened to turn chaos into the enormously ordered system we call the human body! Some of the events recorded in this book are so far beyond the possibility of being coincidences that honest hearts will happily declare that our God is real and that He still rules in the affairs of man. I know that even some who have declared their atheism will believe when they consider the wonderful works of God.

I decided to write this book because the Lord has called us to declare His wondrous works and mighty acts (Psalm 145:4–6). One generation should share with the next the things that God has done. I don't want to leave this present life without doing so. Any atheist who reads what God has done in our lives and the lives of others whom my wife and I have known, will be forced to conclude one of two things: 1) God is real, or 2) I am a liar. As you read these testimonies of His greatness and goodness, maybe you will begin to recall mighty things that the Lord has done in your own life. For those whose eyes and hearts are open, the Lord is still, today, in the business of giving us infallible proofs of the reality of His resurrection and His everlasting life. He is willing to do so in the lives of those who are willing to receive them.

CHAPTER 2

God Plans Every Detail of Our Lives

In 1977, I was an assistant pastor in a small church in up-state New York when the Lord spoke to my wife and me that He was going to bring a change to our ministry. The church granted us a two-month leave of absence during which we planned to travel from New York to Florida, continue to California, and make an entire circuit of the United States before returning home. We thought that, along the way, the Lord might open the door He had chosen for us.

Some months prior to our journey, a missionary from Guatemala visited our church. For the purposes of this story, I will call him Charles. He asked me if I would be willing to go to Guatemala for ten days to minister in several churches. I was not really interested in doing so, but I told him that we would pray about it.

A short time later, someone approached me and said that the Lord had spoken that He would provide $1,780 for our trip to Guatemala. For four reasons, I immediately shelved this message somewhere far back in my mind.

First, it seemed to me that this message was far too precise to be believable. After all, who did this person think they were—a prophetic giant like Isaiah or Elijah who received such precise messages from the Lord?

Second, to economize, we were planning to drive our car and camp throughout the entire trip. We had already come up with a budget. We were certain that we would not need more than about $950. Remember that the dollar of 1977 purchased four or five times what it purchases today (2019).

The third reason that I shelved the prediction that we would have $1,780 for our trip was that as an assistant pastor, I was earning $100 a week. We had a number of financial commitments to resolve before leaving, and the idea of having so much money remaining after our expenses simply did not compute. Our policy has always been to never allow ourselves to become spiritual beggars. We have never been willing to let people know our needs so that they will help us.

Fourth, in no way did we consider our trip to be a trip to Guatemala. To our way of thinking, if we ended up deciding to go to Guatemala, our trip down through Mexico and back up to Texas would only be a little detour from the main purpose of our journey.

The person who spoke to us about God's provision for our trip to Guatemala simply did not understand that we had already been missionaries in the jungles of the Philippines for three years with our four small children. In our hearts, we felt that we had paid our dues, so to speak, in the area of missions. We had no plans whatsoever of ever again being missionaries. We believed that our call was to the good old U.S.A.

During the next few months, the Lord did two things. He spoke to our hearts that He wanted us to accept the invitation to minister in Guatemala, and He also did many miracles of provision. That happened without anyone knowing about our financial needs, and many who gave did not even know that we were planning a trip. When we pulled away from our home in New York to begin our trip, the furthest thing from my mind was the message that the "prophetic giant" had given to us. My wife and I knew that the Lord had abundantly provided for our trip, but we did not know to what degree.

We had money in four different forms: travelers checks, personal checks that had been given to us, cash, and money in a bank account. As I was pulling away from the curb, I asked my wife to add up the different sums to see what the Lord had provided. I cannot express the awe that came over both of us when the total was $1,780 to the penny! At that point, the word we were given should have taken on a deeper meaning for us. That word was "God is going to provide $1,780 for your trip to Guatemala." Yet we still filtered out the idea of this being a "trip to Guatemala." We knew better! We were on a trip throughout the U.S. to discover where the Lord wanted to plant us within the borders of our own country.

Our first primary destination, as we traveled south, was a Christian conference in Florida. We didn't know anyone involved, but a friend had recommended that we pass by. Upon arriving, we set up our tent in a camping area with other tents. We then surveyed our surroundings. To our horror, the place was infested with snakes, primarily with deadly poisonous water moccasins. They lived in a pond that was on the property.

That night we attended the first camp meeting and to our horror, again, the place was also infested with demons. We didn't actually see them, but there were signs of their activity on every hand, and both of us were independently aware of them. When we returned to our tent, we stepped inside, zipped up the door, and looked at each other. I don't remember who expressed his or her feelings first, but we were in complete agreement—"In the morning we will pack up our tent, and we are out of here!"

No sooner had we agreed than the Lord spoke to us both, again independently. He said, "You are not to leave. I want you to stay for the entire time. I have a reason for you being here." We knew that the Lord was speaking clearly when we shared this with each other and realized that we had heard exactly the same message. We obeyed.

During the following days, we met the main speaker of the conference. He was a good man who had a good spirit. I will call him John. We had an extended time of fellowship with him during those days. He pastored a church in Florida, but his church had given him a one-year leave of absence to travel throughout Latin America to minister. He was leaving from that conference to begin his one-year trip. He and his wife would be staying in the camper that they were pulling. We ended up leaving that conference without knowing God's purpose in keeping us there against our own "better judgment," which is often against God's "better judgment."

When we arrived in Texas, we met Charles, the missionary who had invited us to minister in Guatemala for ten days. The plan was to follow him as we both drove south through Mexico to Guatemala. Upon arriving in Guatemala, we ministered in a number of churches there, as planned. However, with the passing of each day, my spirit sank ever deeper into the slough of despond and despair. The spiritual condition of the churches was worse than anything I had faced in my ministry. My wife and I both saw that there was a very dark spiritual cloud over the entire country.

It is hard to express in words the spiritual devastation that I felt in my own heart, as a result of the condition of the churches and the death that it brought to my own heart. Suffice it to say that on the last day of our time in Guatemala, I cried out to the Lord and said, "Lord, now I know what the change will be in our ministry that you spoke to us about in New York. I am returning to the U.S. and going back into business, and I will never preach again, because I am too devastated!"

The Lord then spoke to me in an almost audible voice. He said, "Do you want to die with the rich man? I don't want you to return to the U.S. and tell them about the terrible spiritual condition of Guatemala's churches. Rather, I want you to tell them *why* the churches here are in this condition. Latin America is like the poor man, Lazarus, who lay at the gates of the rich man, hoping for a few crumbs from the rich man's table. The United States has been the rich man both spiritually and naturally, and Latin America has been lying at his gates, looking for a few spiritual crumbs." The Lord then spoke something that we never could have expected. He continued, "From time to time ministers come to visit Latin America and throw out a few crumbs of blessing, and then they return to the U.S. Are you willing to come to live here and give them your best?"

Heaven's grace always comes with heaven's Word. Although my heart shrank back at the very thought, I responded, "Lord, I am willing to bring my wife and four children to this place only if You make Your calling to us so clear that we will have no doubt whatsoever."

The next morning, we departed to drive through Mexico and continue our planned trip through the U.S. Our next major stop was a conference in California. We had never before attended that conference, and knew almost no one there. While there, we asked some leaders to pray for us, explaining that we had a major decision to make, but we did not tell them what the decision involved. A small group of ministers gathered around us to pray. One of them was from New Zealand. We had never heard of him, and he certainly had never heard of people so insignificant as us. As they finished praying, this man said to us, "While we were praying, I saw written over your heads the word 'Guatemala.' I assume that you have just come back from Guatemala, but you will return there."

I had told the Lord that if He made His call for us to go to Guatemala so clear that we could not mistake it, that I would be willing to move my family there. Imagine that this came from a total stranger! This was the first in a series of incredibly sovereign and supernatural events that confirmed our call to Guatemala in such a way that my wife and I knew beyond any doubt that we were to go and live there. We finally understood why this had all begun with a prophetic word that God would provide $1,780 for our trip to Guatemala. It turned out that Guatemala was not a small detour in God's main plan! It was the whole purpose of the trip!

One year and three months later we were living in Guatemala. We had rented a house a short distance from Charles' home. One day he called to tell me that a missionary from Costa Rica had arrived at his house to stay for a day on his way to the U.S. for a time of rest. I will call this missionary Ralph. Charles knew that my wife and I also knew Ralph, so he invited us to his house for an evening of fellowship.

While there, the two men were talking about old times when they had both ministered together in Ralph's Bible school in Costa Rica. Then, to my amazement, one of them asked the other if he knew where John was. I excitedly asked them, "Do you know John?" They said, "Oh yes, he used to come and teach in our Bible school in Costa Rica." I explained that I had met him a year and three months before in Florida. I told them, "I am sure that he is pastoring his church again in Florida because a year and three months ago, the church there gave him their approval for him to be absent for a year." We dropped the subject there.

The next morning, I had to do an errand in downtown Guatemala City, by far the largest city in Central America. It had about one and a half million inhabitants at that time, and three million in 2019. I called Charles and asked him if he and Ralph would like to accompany me on my errand so we could continue our fellowship. They agreed to do so. Two other persons joined us.

On the way, Ralph said to me, "Marvin, would you mind stopping by such and such a building on your way downtown? I want to buy Mexican auto insurance from an office there for our trip through Mexico." Although the high-rise office building he mentioned was not on the route I normally took, it was on a route that led to the same place I needed to go. I told him that I would be happy to do so.

When we arrived at the parking lot that the high-rise office building used, I said to Charles, "Why don't you take Ralph into the insurance agent's office, because there is no need for all five of us to crowd into his small office." Charles said, "Oh, it's not small at all. It is very large, so we can all go."

One of the incredible "coincidences" in this whole scenario is that I had made a short trip to Mexico just three weeks before, for which I had bought auto insurance from precisely this same agent. Just by coincidence the previous location of the office had been changed just three weeks before, a day or two before I purchased insurance. It was moved from a very large area into a very small one. I explained this to Charles who responded, "Since I do not know where the new office is located, why don't you and Ralph go there alone. We will wait for you." I agreed to do so.

As we walked through the glass doors of that very modern high-rise office complex and approached the elevators, who was coming off the elevator? None other but John whom we had met in Florida! When he saw me, he exclaimed, "This is God's doing! I just cancelled my Guatemalan auto insurance, and I was planning to depart early in the morning to return to the U.S. However, I am leaving with a heavy heart. I have been ministering to a group of Guatemalan businessmen who are hungry for the Lord, but there is no one to teach them. There is no one to lead them on. I am going to delay my trip one day and call a meeting with them tonight. I will introduce you to them, and have you teach them tonight to see if they would like you to continue teaching them."

We met that night, and the Lord did a work in the hearts of those businessmen. They asked if I would be willing to teach them each week. I told them that I was willing and that they could choose the time and place. For the next year we met with the group, and the group grew.

One of the men who had been added to the group said to me after one of the meetings, "We cannot survive spiritually on one meeting a week." I responded, "My family and I meet together every Sunday morning in our home at 10:00 a.m. You are welcome to join us."

The next Sunday morning, at five minutes before 10:00 a.m., there was a knock on the door. That man, his wife, and their infant daughter had come to meet with us. The next week others joined, and the group kept growing until we had to rent a place for the meetings. This is how the Lord began the local church in Guatemala where my wife and I have had a home for over 40 years. Others of the businessmen's families also joined.

What the Fool Says in His Heart

"The fool hath said in his heart, There is no God" (Psalm 14:1). If we consider the list of coincidences in this chain of events and the fruit that those coincidences produced, it is safe to conclude that only a fool would attribute all this to mere chance. If only one of the many details had not coincided, we may not have enjoyed the fruit that God wished to give. While the details are too many to number, consider a few:

Inner Promptings and Decisions

1. A friend in New York told us about the conference in Florida and encouraged us to stop by.

2. God prompted my wife and me to remain at the Florida conference until the end even though we both would have preferred leaving. If we had departed, we would not have met John, who was to introduce us to the Guatemalan businessmen.

3. Once in Guatemala, I needed Mexican auto insurance three weeks before Ralph did, and I chose to purchase it from a specific company.

4. Three weeks later, I happened to invite Charles and Ralph to go with me on my errand.

5. Ralph had independently chosen to buy insurance from the same company that I had used and asked me to stop by their office.

6. Since two extra people joined the three of us who were going downtown, it became obvious that I needed to suggest that only two of us should go into the small insurance office. There would have been no need to suggest this if only three of us had been in the car, because the office was big enough for three, but not five.

7. The insurance agency was in the process of moving to a different office at the precise time that I was there three weeks before. Therefore, I knew where the new location was, while Charles did not. That led him to suggest that I, rather than he, should go to the office with Ralph.

Precise Timings

1. Ralph "just happened" to arrive at Charles' house the day before John would be coming out of the insurance office. Without going into further details, there were many divine appointments that even caused me to know Ralph personally.

2. I decided to run an errand downtown on the very day that John was at the insurance agency.

3. Our path was guided through the traffic of a city of one and a half million inhabitants, through just the right number of traffic light stops for us to arrive at the doors of the building the very second John was exiting the elevators. If we had arrived literally 60 seconds sooner or later,

I would have missed meeting up with John. Coming to know him in the Florida convention, was the very reason that the Lord wanted us to remain there, even though we wanted to leave.

4. John and I crossed paths in Guatemala a year and three months after we met, at a place almost 2,500 miles away by land, and our meeting was vitally linked to our future ministry in Guatemala.

The fact that two other men came with us, which led to Charles' suggestion that I, rather than he, go to the office with Ralph was a small but absolutely essential detail for God's purposes to be fulfilled. If only three of us would have travelled, all three would have met John, who would have put Charles in contact with the businessmen instead of me. John had known Charles for many years and knew he had every advantage: he was completely bilingual, had grown up in Latin America as a son of missionaries, and was an excellent Bible teacher. John had spent enough time with me in Florida to know that I spoke barely enough Spanish to communicate the most basic matters, and that I would need a translator to teach those men. Why wouldn't the Lord want Charles to be chosen instead of me? That would have been *my* choice!

The Lord alone knew that six months later Charles would fall into immorality and leave Guatemala and the ministry. Nothing permanent would have come from our divinely appointed meeting with John. Yet some would say that all of this was merely coincidence. No wonder the Bible declares that the *fool* says in his heart that there is no God!

What if our friend had not told us about the conference in Florida? What if John had not been the main speaker or had not been leaving to travel on a trip that would take him a year and three months? What if we had not heard the voice that told us to remain in the conference or had ignored it? Who was it who knew that the hearts of the people would be moved to give us exactly $1,780 and that it was for our trip to Guatemala, *not* primarily for our trip through the U.S.?

God's leading that controlled each one of these "what ifs" has borne fruit which continues to this day. It includes, not only a church, but an orphanage that we had for many years, a ministerial training institute, a K–12 homeschooling curriculum in Spanish, a fellowship of over 120 churches, and ministerial institutes by extension in many other places of the world. God knows what He is doing! If we would only allow Him to lead us through this short life!

God still does mighty miracles in the lives of His people. The fool is too blind to recognize God's hand at work and attributes it all to coincidence when he is forced to see it. Maybe we are not fools who say that there is no God, but are we blinded to some degree to the wonderful things that the Lord does for us day after day? Let's pray that the Lord will open our eyes to see the wonderful works that He is daily doing in our lives!

The Bible declares that "the very hairs of your head are all numbered" (Matthew 10:30). Since we know that our God is aware of such minute details, and since we know that He rules in the affairs of man (Daniel 4:17), how can we live day after day without recognizing the wonderful and sovereign works that He does continually in our lives? Lord, open our eyes to see Your glory revealed continually in the earth and in our lives!

CHAPTER 3

A Time for Every Purpose

King Solomon, the wisest man in history, wrote that there is "a time for every purpose under heaven" (Ecclesiastes 3:1 NKJV). Through a life-changing event, this truth was made real to my wife and me when we first arrived in Guatemala as missionaries. It began with a word from God.

The Lord's true voice always brings His presence, as Elijah's experience teaches us (1 Kings 19:12). If the voice we hear brings a deep awareness of His true presence, we are likely hearing the Lord's voice. However, I am rarely 100 percent sure that I am hearing from the Lord rather than my own heart or even the enemy. I also have strong doubts about the spiritual condition of people who display great confidence in their ability to hear God's voice and who act and talk as if their ability were infallible. I am cautious about the messages they claim to have received. The problem is that many have difficulty discerning the difference between God's presence and an emotional high produced by their own soul. For me, the proof of whether or not I have truly heard the Lord's voice lies in the fruit that follows.

One day, when we first arrived in Guatemala, I decided to work on our car to attempt to find and resolve a small problem.

I went outside, opened the hood, and began to work. At that moment, I felt the Lord saying, "It is not time to work on your car. It is time to pray." I obeyed that still small voice that brought with it a consciousness of His presence.

The next day, I was in my office praying, and I heard the Lord's still small voice again. It was not until after I had experienced the events I am about to share here—the fruit of that voice—that I could say with certainty that the voice I heard on both days was the Lord's. This new message was surprising. He said, "Go out and work on your car. It is not time to pray." Again, I obeyed. I knew that there is a time for every purpose under heaven. I saw the problem as soon as I opened the car's hood: a small part was broken. I would have to buy a new part at the car dealership. I immediately left home in another vehicle that we had. The timing between the moment when I heard His voice and discovered the faulty part, and the moment when I departed for the car dealership was sovereignly led by the Lord.

A Terrible Airplane Crash

I was almost at the dealership when I saw a small airplane cross the six-lane boulevard that I was on. I knew that I was near Guatemala's international airport, so neither the sight of the airplane, nor the fact that it was descending was surprising to me. I assumed that it was about to land.

What I did not realize until a moment later was that it had just *departed* from the airport and had flown beyond the end of the runway! It was, indeed, about to land, but not at the airport. Rather, it was descending into a densely populated section of Guatemala City. About 30 seconds later, it hit the top of a four-story building and broke in half. The front half, with two people, fell into the parking lot of that building, and the back half, with two other people, catapulted over a wall and onto the street, *right in front of my vehicle*. Both parts were in flames. It was the biggest fire I had ever seen in my life.

I later learned that those on board were four missionaries. They had just filled their tanks to capacity with gasoline, and had taken off en route to Mexico. Upon lifting off, they lost power and could not maintain altitude. The pilot was trying to reach the boulevard I was on, hoping to land on it. He only had to clear the four-story building that was in his way. He almost made it. He lacked only five to ten feet of altitude to reach his goal when he hit the very top of the fourth story.

Afterward, a friend of ours whose husband was also a pilot told us that she was in the airport bathroom on that fateful day. She talked there with the wife of the pilot who crashed, just before she took off with her husband. She said to our friend, "Oh, how I long to be with the Lord!" A few moments later, her longing was granted, and she was with the One whom she so loved and longed for! God's ways are not our ways! Solomon said that there is a time for every purpose, including "a time to be born and a time to die" (Ecclesiastes 3:2). Some of her last words were a testimony that she was ready to die and meet the Lord. Do you have that testimony today? You can have it if you accept the reality of Jesus Christ and the sacrifice He made to save you from eternal damnation.

I was about 60 yards from the busiest intersection in Guatemala City and so close to the crash site that although almost everyone in that intersection stopped and approached the horrific scene, I was among the first there. The crash occurred so close to my vehicle that when I walked up to the site, not a single person stood between me and the flames that surrounded the two dead bodies before me.

I Heard God's Voice Coming Out of the Flames

As I stood there, the Lord began to speak to me in a very clear way. Again, I can now say that it was the Lord because a good part of what He spoke to me was later fulfilled. I will share part of His message here. However, I first want to mention that if I had not heard and obeyed His voice about praying instead of working on my car, I wouldn't have been at that crash. I would have driven to the car dealership the day before. Also, if I hadn't obeyed the instruction to work on my car instead of praying, I would not have witnessed one of the most horrible and awesome events in my life.

In no way do I say this to bring glory to myself or claim that I have a great ability to hear God's voice. I have learned over and over that our life in Christ is all of grace. I have learned that He can speak to and through any donkey that He chooses, as he did with Balaam. When I hear the voice of the Lord, I recognize that His word has fallen on my ear through a sovereign act of His grace, and not because of my importance or great spirituality.

This crash was both horrible and wonderful. It was horrible beyond words, but it was also wonderful for at least two reasons: 1) the Lord heard the cry of the pilot's wife and, at that moment, brought her eternal soul into the rest that she longed for; 2) at the crash site, the Lord spoke to me some glorious things about Guatemala and about our own lives. Many of them have come to pass.

A Mighty Visitation Is at Hand

I continued to observe the wreckage and hear the Lord's voice for about 20 minutes. By then, ambulances had removed the dead passengers. When I turned around to return to my vehicle, I witnessed something I shall never forget. During those 20 minutes, at least 20,000 people had gathered to view the disaster. The busiest intersection of the city was surrounded by office buildings and businesses. People had come out of those buildings onto the street and also onto the roofs of the buildings, out of their vehicles onto the boulevard, and up onto the large elevated grassy areas and gardens surrounding that enormous intersection. The area was packed with people in all directions and at many levels.

While there, the last thing I heard the Lord say was, "Multitudes have gathered here because they have been brought face-to-face with the reality of death and destruction. I will gather multitudes in this nation by bringing them face-to-face with the reality of resurrection life and My presence that will raise the dead and heal the sick before their eyes." I knew that He was speaking about bringing to Guatemala one of the greatest revivals that the world has ever witnessed. This has not yet happened, but at this writing we are 40 years closer to that visitation. I have a deep conviction that it is at the door, and my conviction is based on sound evidence.

The world will soon hear about God's goodness to Guatemala, as He turns the nation from violence, the grip of drug lords, murders, kidnappings, robbery, and every sort of vice and corruption. Soon, it will be a nation that is known throughout the world as a people who are under the favor of the Resurrected Lord and Redeemer. The vilest of sinners will forsake their evil ways as they turn to Him. Repentance will even reach the drug lords throughout the nation, and it will reach the very citadels of power, including the National Palace.

I am certain that Guatemala is not the only country in the world that will be visited in a glorious way. Wherever we live, we can be a person who cries out to the Lord for His visitation in our own lives and in our own nation. He will hear that cry, and He will respond.

Guatemala and Israel

I was not surprised when the Lord spoke this to me about Guatemala. Even before we had moved there, He had given me a verse that summarizes what He will do in Guatemala. It is Jeremiah 33:9 (quoted below the next heading). Although Jeremiah is speaking primarily about what the Lord will do in Israel, for some reason the Lord has forged a link between Guatemala and Israel. One reason may well be because of what the president of Guatemala did in 1947.

The world had just discovered that 6 million Jews had perished in the Holocaust. In spite of this, not enough member-nations in the United Nations considered those Jewish lives to be sufficient cause to warrant the establishment of a Jewish State where the Jewish people could live in peace. The president of Guatemala, Juan José Arévalo, loved the Jews and asked one of the most eloquent men in Guatemala, Jorge García Granados, to accept an appointment to the U.N. as Guatemala's ambassador. The president gave the new ambassador a charge—to persuade the Latin American nations to vote yes for the formation of a Jewish nation.

In November of 1947, in spite of the millions of Jews who had died, most nations of the world were still not willing to permit the Jews to form their own nation in the Holy Land.

In the United Nations, the requirement for the General Assembly to cast a vote was that one of the members would have to make a motion to vote on any given issue, and then another member would have to second the motion.

In May of 1948, there was not even one nation that was willing to make a motion to vote regarding the formation of a Jewish State. After many days of indecision, only one hour remained before the expiration of the allotted time that had been set to either decide or else remove that issue from the agenda of the U.N.

Suddenly, President Truman from the United States sent a message to his U.N. ambassador ordering him to make a motion to vote. Immediately after his motion, the ambassador from Guatemala seconded the motion, and the vote was taken. The General Assembly voted to approve the establishment of the State of Israel. From then until today, the Jewish nation has had a very close relationship with Guatemala.[3]

---

3   https://revistaindustria.com/2009/06/jun-09-israel-y-guatemala-articulo-18-israel-
     y-guatemala-a-61-anos-de-la-proclamacion-de-la-independencia-de-israel-por-el-
     lider-sionista-david-ben-gurion-israel-ha-enfrentado-guerras-y-una-cont/.

The Blessing That Is at the Door

The Lord has promised that those who bless Israel will be blessed (Genesis 12:3). From what the Lord has spoken to others and myself, Guatemala is going to receive at least one of the blessings that He pronounces over Israel. It is found in Jeremiah 33:9:

> *"It shall be to me a name of joy, a praise and an honour before all the nations of the earth, which shall hear all the good that I do unto them: and they shall fear and tremble for all the goodness and for all the prosperity that I procure unto it."*

The Lord has spoken to several people that this blessing will come upon Guatemala. Even before moving to Guatemala, the Lord spoke to me in a very clear way that He would fulfill in Guatemala the many details found in Jeremiah 33, and not only in Israel.

Later, when we were living in Guatemala, we were invited to attend a monthly meeting of Guatemalan missionaries. A different missionary shared each month. The first time we attended, a missionary shared whom I had never met, and who had been in Guatemala for many years. He testified that the previous summer he and his wife were visiting the U.S. They were discouraged, and as they considered not returning to Guatemala, he said to the Lord, "Lord, if You are going to do anything in Guatemala, please give me a Scripture that explains what you will do." My wife and I had not shared our vision for Guatemala with anyone. We were awestruck when he said, "The Lord gave me Jeremiah 33 and said that this is what He will do in Guatemala."

About two years later, a young woman from New Zealand spent a few days with us. She was planning on being a missionary in another Latin American country. We had never met her, but someone we knew recommended that we receive her. We did not share a single thing with her about our vision for

Guatemala. Maybe one reason was that she had felt a call to minister in another country, and we did not want to make her feel bad about not being called to Guatemala.

During her time with us, I asked her if she ever shared messages with the churches she visited. When she responded in the affirmative, I invited her to speak in our church the following Sunday. During that meeting, as I was translating for her, she suddenly stopped in the middle of her message and declared, "I have a message from God for this nation. It is Jeremiah 33:9." She then read that verse and continued on with her message that was completely unrelated to that verse. Of course, my heart was almost bursting with joy at the further confirmation of God's promise. God will do great things in Guatemala because of His grace and also because Guatemala blessed Israel. Do *you* bless Israel, at least in your heart and your prayers? If you do, God has promised to bless you also (Genesis 12:3).

CHAPTER 4

My Times Are in Your Hands

Back at the Airplane Crash

Over the years the Lord has emphasized to us the importance of the first words He speaks in the Book of Revelation. He said to John, "I am Alpha and Omega, the beginning and the ending" (Revelation 1:8). He doesn't say here that He is *in* the beginning or that He is *in* the end. Rather, He *is* the beginning, and He *is* the end. Since He has also told us that He never changes (Hebrews 13:8), this means that the beginning and the end are the same. These first words of Jesus in Revelation are one of the greatest keys to understanding the book, and He repeats them five times in the book.

In our Bible school, we have a course called "The Relationship between the Beginning and the End." We learn from that course that everything God begins, He ends in the same way He began it. In all of His works, He gives mankind a revelation of His Son, both at the beginning and ending of every divine work.

The Lord spoke something else to me while I stood at the scene of the airplane crash. He told me that, during our time in Guatemala, we would personally experience the reality of the One who is the beginning and end. He said, "Your time in Guatemala has begun with an airplane crash, and your time in Guatemala will end with an airplane crash." He opened my spiritual eyes to see a commercial jet, one that carries about 100 passengers, crashing in Guatemala.

Another Airplane Crash

When we arrived in Guatemala, I did not know a single word of Spanish. When people poured out their hearts with tears about a problem, I would often have to ask them, "Will you repeat what you said? I did not understand you." In 1984, more than six years after the Lord spoke to me about how our time in Guatemala would end, I walked into my office one morning. and the Lord was there to meet me in a special way. I felt burned-out as a minister and missionary. I often spent eight to ten hours a day studying Spanish. I had been pastoring all those years in a language that I barely knew. The spiritual and natural burdens had been tremendous.

On top of this, from the time that the Lord supernaturally called me to the ministry at the age of 12, I never wanted to be in the ministry. When I would read Hebrews 5:4 about the honor of being in the ministry, I would often say to the Lord, "Lord, this is an honor that I do not want."

I thought that the honor Hebrews refers to was to stand before people and preach to them. I had a hidden longing in my heart to leave the ministry and return to business. This was not my way of rejecting the Lord or His way. I loved to seek the Lord. In fact, my idea was to be in a successful business where I could spend most of my time seeking the Lord, and where I would never have to preach again unless a message was really burning in my heart. I did not want my reason to preach again to be simply that another church service had come, and I was the preacher.

When I walked into my office that morning, the presence of the Lord was there. He spoke to me and said, "I want you to move to Dallas and open a bakery." This kind of business had interested me for many years. Two years before, in 1982, I had sensed that Americans were hungry for top-quality chocolate chip cookies. My idea was right. Mrs. Fields began to sell her cookies that very year (something that I did not know at the time; few people had even heard of her). Others did the same, and the chocolate chip cookie business soon mushroomed to a five-billion-dollar-a-year business.

My mother made homemade bread throughout all of her married life. One day, when I was a boy, she gave a loaf to a neighbor who had just given birth. Later, the neighbor asked my mother if she could buy bread from her on a continual basis. Many other neighbors heard about it and did the same. Within weeks, she was selling so much bread that she had the funds to rent a building, buy equipment, and begin a bakery. In those days, bakeries that made specialty breads were rare, and it was rare to find a place that sold homemade bread.

The week that my mother planned on opening her business, my father lost his employment, and we had to live for some time on the money she had saved. That ended her plans for a bakery. I have always believed that the Lord saved our family from riches that would almost certainly have brought us spiritual shipwreck. Afterward, throughout our married life, my wife Barbara has also baked excellent homemade bread. So, the idea of a bakery was not at all foreign to me.

When I heard God's voice, I called my wife, who was teaching our children, and told her what I had heard. Without hesitation she asked, "But what about the Lord saying that there would be an airplane crash at the end of our time in Guatemala?" It was as though she had been thinking about that every day. The truth is that almost never did either of us think about that word. As soon as she asked, both of us were shocked because we remembered the news of the previous day, news we heard because the airport runway was less than a mile from our home in a direct line. A four-engine airplane had taken off and crashed in the city, killing everyone on board.

A House and a Bakery

I won't go into the details of how the Lord further confirmed our decision to go to Dallas, but there were no fewer than 40 ways that He used to confirm that we were doing His will. We moved to Dallas, intending to rent a house and begin the bakery. As I waited for assistance in the lobby of a real estate agency, a woman who was also waiting began to tell me her horror story. She had moved to Dallas, for work purposes, three months before. There was such a housing shortage in Dallas that she had been sleeping in her car for three months. She said, "There is no way that you are going to find a house in or around this city." But as she talked, the Lord said to me, "I will give you a house today." He granted that miracle, and we rented the perfect house for us in a very nice neighborhood that very day.

A couple days later, we happened to go into a bakery and sandwich shop to get a snack. As we were sitting there, the owner's wife happened to approach us, and we began to talk. When she found out that we were planning to go into the bakery business, she said, "Would you like to buy this bakery? My husband is trying to sell it." It was in a perfect location on one of the main thoroughfares of Dallas. We talked with the owner and his price was reasonable. Within two weeks of arriving in Dallas we were the owners of a bakery.

We gave a very large down payment, and the closing date was set for about 10 days later. At the end of those ten days, my wife and I were exhausted from all the work involved in learning the details of the bakery and from getting settled in our newly rented house. The night before the closing of the deal, we spent a few minutes seeking the Lord before falling into bed. As we did so, the Lord opened my eyes to a very clear vision. I saw two roads leading from my present position. One led downward and became darker as it descended. The word "business" was written on it. The other road led upward and became brighter as it ascended. The word "ministry" was written on it.

The moment I saw the vision, a divine understanding entered my heart regarding what the real honor of the ministry truly is. The honor is not to stand before men. Rather, the honor is to stand before God and to dedicate ourselves to eternal values.

Instantly I repented. I said, "Lord forgive me for rejecting the ministry and its honor. I will joyfully stand before anyone, anywhere, anytime, and minister in Your name as long as I also have the privilege of standing before You to give my life to eternal values. But Lord, what do I do now? Tomorrow I am supposed to give the rest of the money for the purchase of the bakery."

The Lord responded immediately. He said, "It is up to you." I asked, "But Lord, what about the down payment that we gave? We will probably lose it." Again, He responded, "I said, 'It is up to you.' " At that moment, I remembered the prophetic word that came to King Amaziah after he had foolishly given 100 talents of silver (almost $3 million in 2019) to hire mercenaries for a war he faced. When he decided not to use them because of a rebuke from a man of God, he asked that man of God, "But what about the 100 talents I gave?" As the Lord's words rang in my ears, I remembered his answer: "The Lord is able to give thee much more than this" (2 Chronicles 25:9).

A Great Debt Was Incurred

I made my decision. The next morning I would tell the previous owner that I had decided not to buy. We had borrowed the money for the down payment, and at that time, we had very little income. We received just enough to meet our needs with four children. Today, our income at that time would be considered an income well below the poverty level. If we would have given half of our income every month towards the debt, it would have taken us over 6 years to pay it off. We knew that, without a miracle, it would be impossible to pay that debt for many years. When my wife and I married, almost 20 years before, I had a small student debt, but by this time we had lived debt-free for almost all of our married life. It seemed that we would now be deeply in debt for many years, with no apparent way to pay it off.

I want to emphasize here that I am in no way sharing this experience to say that being in business will lead a person into darkness. The Lord was dealing with a specific issue in my *own* life—my unwillingness to be in the ministry and my unthankfulness for His call on my life. He made it clear that I am called to the ministry and not to business. Others are called by the Lord to be in business and not in the ministry. Some have the freedom to do both, as Paul the apostle had, at least for a time.

The next morning, when I told the owner what my decision was, he looked up at me from his desk and said, "Well you won't get the down payment back. I am keeping it!" I said to him, "You know that I am in the ministry, and if you feel that you can keep that money and have God's blessing, that is your decision." We went to the lawyer to cancel the deal, and he kept the money. It is always risky to take that which does not belong to us, whether it be nothing more than a pencil or millions of dollars. In either case, it is robbery. Exactly one year later, that owner was in bankruptcy. He owed $750,000, ten times what he had taken from us. And the banks moved into his business and physically removed all of his equipment.

A Great Debt Was Paid

In complete honesty before the Lord, my wife and I have no idea how we ended up paying that debt, even though this sounds ludicrous. What we *do* remember is what the Lord spoke to us after we had incurred that debt. He said that many people spend their lives in debt because they are not serious about getting free of their debts. For example, people often reason this way: "Well, I owe a tremendous amount of money, so what difference will it make if I go to the restaurant and spend $30?"

It is true that $30 is insignificant compared to the debt of many, but it is definitely significant for the Lord. It sends Him a message that this person is not really serious about getting out of debt.

The Lord spoke to us that if we would show Him that we were serious about paying off our debt, He would help us. He asked us to tighten our belts and apply everything we could toward the debt. We obeyed and in one year we were debt-free again! Once again, we refused to turn into spiritual beggars. No one ever knew that we had that debt except the one who had loaned it to us. We did not receive large amounts of money from a small number of people. Rather, it was here a little and there a little. This is why we do not know how it ended up being paid, but before we knew it, the debt was paid. God is faithful!

The Airplane Crash that I Saw in the Vision

A short time after I had sincerely embraced the ministry for the first time in my life, we returned to Guatemala. Over two years before, in 1982, I had become a pilot, and I continued to fly after our return to Guatemala. However, although I had my license from the U.S., because I was flying an airplane that was registered in Guatemala, the country required me to also receive instruction from Guatemalan pilots and obtain a Guatemalan license.

I got to know a number of very good Guatemalan pilots, but the closest one was Carlos, whose full name I will not disclose. For many years, he was the chief pilot of the Guatemalan national airline. He had received instruction from the U.S.

air force, and he also graduated first in his class at Eastern Airlines (one of the largest airlines in the U.S. for many years until it ceased operations in January 1991). He was the only pilot in Guatemala who was authorized to give check rides in commercial jetliners to approve other pilots to fly them.

Carlos flew with me and instructed me for many hours. On two occasions, he flew with me from Guatemala to Miami, Florida, in the plane that had been made available to our ministry. I should add here that I, personally, did not have the financial wherewithal to fly airplanes, but the airplane had been provided for our ministry at no cost to me.

When we returned from Dallas to Guatemala, I continued to be in contact with Carlos. The national airline had been sold, and he lost his job as chief pilot. At this point, he was one of the owners of an airplane shuttle service based at the Guatemalan airport. They grew to the place where they could buy a used 100-seat commercial jet. I was at the airport the day before it was scheduled to make its maiden flight with paying passengers.

The pilot who was to be the flight engineer on the next day's flight asked me if I would like to see the flight deck of their jet. Of course, I accepted his offer. My friend Carlos was to be the pilot in command the next day, and I also knew the man who was to act as co-pilot on the flight. I had received instruction from him also.

The next day we received the horrific news. As they were attempting to land in northern Guatemala, they were in the clouds and the plane had flown straight into a mountain. All 100 people and crew died. I was devastated for a number of reasons. One, my friend Carlos had died. Two, my wife and I knew his wife, and we were devastated for her sake. Three, I had absolutely no doubt that this 100-seat jet was precisely the jet I had seen crashing over Guatemala in the vision I had had while standing in front of the first crash where the missionaries had died seven years before.

I was dumbfounded when I realized that I had not only been inside that very airplane the day before, but that I personally knew all three pilots on board. How could the Lord have called my attention to this event and the fulfillment of the vision in any clearer way? Who would have believed, seven years before, when I had that vision, that I would personally know the pilots, that I would be onboard the airplane that I saw crashing, on the day before it would crash, and that I would be a friend of the captain?

But I felt devastated for another, more personal reason. At the moment I saw that vision seven years before, the Lord said to me, "Your time in Guatemala has begun with an airplane crash, and your time in Guatemala will end with an airplane crash." As a family, we had just returned to Guatemala about a week before this happened. I went into my office and cried out to the Lord. I prayed, "Lord, I have no doubt that this is the crash you were showing to me seven years ago. But we just came back, and now you are saying that our time here is over! What should we do?"

As I was crying out to the Lord, a verse came to me. That verse is, "My times are in thy hand . . ." (Psalm 31:15). As is almost always the case, receiving a vision, dream, or a word from the Lord is only the first step in understanding the message that He wants to give us. Next, we need understanding and/or we must receive an interpretation of what we have seen or heard. The Lord told this truth to Aaron and Miriam when they rose up against Moses. He told them that He gives dreams, visions, and dark sayings to the prophets, but that with Moses He spoke plainly, face to face (Numbers 12:6–8). Dreams, visions, and dark sayings have one thing in common—they all need an interpretation.

A New Time in Guatemala

The instant that verse came to my heart, I realized that "times" refers to a season or a period of time, and the Hebrew confirms this. The Lord then spoke to me, "Your time in Guatemala began with a crash, and it has now ended with a crash. You are now beginning a new time; a new day. It is now time for a new beginning for you in this nation. From this day on things will be different in your ministry."

Once again, the fruit that follows a word from the Lord (or the lack of fruit) is one of the best ways of knowing if we have really heard from the Lord or not. We had spent seven very difficult years in Guatemala. The church had grown so slowly that people on the outside looking in mocked us. One person said to a church member, "God is clearly not with your church, because after seven years you still have only 80 members."

From the day of my friend's crash onward, everything was different in our ministry, just as the Lord said it would be. The church began to grow, and we had to move from one larger place to another. First, we moved from one part of our property to a new enlarged and remodeled chapel. Then, we had to rent an auditorium in the city. When it became too full, we had to have two services on Sunday mornings. We then built a building on our property that holds up to 1,500 people (when packed in).

In addition to this, pastors began to ask if they could walk with our ministry. Also, leaders who had been raised up during those first years were sent out to pastor new churches. Today, in 2019, there are now over 120 churches in 18 nations that are a part of the ministry. Shortly afterward, the Lord led us to open an orphanage, then a grade school and high school, and a ministerial training center that has had about 30 satellite training centers using video and DVD recordings. We now also have a Bible-based kindergarten through 12th grade homeschooling curriculum in Spanish that leads students to the Lord. The curriculum is available on DVD, online, and a good part of the material is interactive. It is being used in over 20 nations.

God has done great things, and all we can do is marvel at His goodness and greatness. We are thankful that He has allowed us to be a part of what He is doing. It is not the fruit of my ministry, but rather the fruit of God's mercy. He wants to show that same mercy in every life that will turn to Him and choose to follow His way instead of their own way. If your heart longs to know Him in a greater way, He longs to reveal Himself to you. You can ask Him to do so at this very moment!

CHAPTER 5

God's Kindness to a Father and His Children

Shortly after moving to Guatemala the first time in 1978 to live there with my family, I received a phone call from the U.S. informing me that my father had died. I went to my office to pour out my heart before the Lord. I did so, not merely out of sadness for losing my father, but because of the terrible scenario that I assumed would unfold during his funeral.

My Father and Uncle Sam

When I was almost ten years of age, my father moved our family from the Pittsburgh, Pennsylvania area to Detroit, Michigan. He did so because there were much better employment opportunities in Detroit. He finished raising his six children in Detroit, back when many parts of the city were beautiful neighborhoods.

Years after all six of us had left home and gotten married, he moved back to Pennsylvania and bought a house that happened to be about one mile from my Uncle Sam who was married to my mother's sister. For decades, my father had rejected

Uncle Sam because of what he stood for. He was one of the 12 main leaders of a small religious cult that had churches in several places in the United States. He was looked upon as a spiritual giant by many relatives on my mother's side of the family, as well as on my father's side. On the other hand, many of those same relatives looked on my father as a spiritual failure. Why?

During the first years of my parents' marriage, my father was a very hard and unkind person. He was quick to enter into fistfights with anyone who offended him. He chewed tobacco, swore, and hated religion. His older sister, Ruth, was a true Christian, who lived in a house that was on the same property, about 50 yards from our house. For years, she prayed earnestly for her younger brother, pleading with the Lord to save his soul. God heard and answered her prayer in an awesome way.

One day, when my father arrived home from his job, he suddenly had a hair-raising, life-changing encounter with eternal realities. His eyes were opened, and he was hanging by a thread over the flames of hell. He began to cry out to my mother, "Call Ruth! Call Ruth! Ask her to come and pray for me!" Of course, Ruth came and prayed, and my father's testimony from that day on was that when he came back from where he had been hanging over hell, and he came to himself, he was leaping with joy and shouting, "It is done! It is done! I am saved!"

From that day until the day of his death, he never had another fistfight, never swore again, and never again chewed tobacco. His hatred for religion turned into a love for the Lord and His ways. He felt that God was calling him to the ministry, but in those days, the church he attended did not encourage its people to enter the ministry, much less provide a way for them to reach that goal. For many years, he felt frustrated and a failure. He had four boys and two girls, and he began to pray that one of his boys would take up the call to the ministry that he had felt and failed to fulfill.

Returning now to the story of the house that he purchased in Pennsylvania, it needed a number of repairs and remodeling. He was well able to do the work since he was a former contractor who built houses. However, some of the work required more than one man, and Uncle Sam was more than willing to help him. Some of us were concerned that Uncle Sam not only had the desire to help him in the natural, but also to win him over to his cult and religious beliefs. Although he did not succeed in doing so, my father came to appreciate his help, and for the first time after many years, they became friends. Of course, our mother was very happy about that, because she was one who considered Uncle Sam to be a spiritual giant.

My Father's Funeral

When I received that phone call in Guatemala, telling me that my father had died, I envisioned a terrible scenario that I assumed would unfold. It was almost certain that my mother would ask Uncle Sam to conduct our father's funeral. I knew that, in the eyes of all the family members on both sides, it would be a kind of final proof that Uncle Sam was a spiritual giant and that our father had been a failure. As I poured out my heart to the Lord, He spoke to me very clearly and said, "Your Uncle Sam will not conduct the funeral of your father, because he will die before the funeral. There will be two funerals." My father's funeral was only two days away, and it was to be held on a weekend, so if this message came from the Lord, my uncle did not have long to live!

I flew the next day to Pittsburgh, and my aunt, Uncle Sam's sister, picked me up from the airport. Literally, the first thing she said to me when I got off the airplane was, "Uncle Sam died today." I knew that God had intervened in a serious and awesome way, but I did not fully understand what God was doing until the two funerals were well under way.

If during a person's life, on just one occasion they believe that they have heard a message from God about the future, and it then happens as they heard, an atheist could attribute this to sheer coincidence. But if this happens many times in a person's life, as is the case with the experiences my wife and I have had, and as I share in this book, only a fool could call them all just mere coincidences. Imagine the enormous significance of hearing that another person, who is healthy, is going to die within two days, and then having it occur. And this is mere coincidence?

Uncle Sam, the spiritual giant, had twelve children, twice as many as my father. They were scattered all over the U.S., from coast to coast, but they were all able to fly in to attend their father's funeral. Then, of course, they also attended our father's funeral. The message that God was giving became very clear to anyone with understanding.

My father had failed to fulfill his call to the ministry. He had prayed for years that one of his four boys would take up that call. God heard that prayer, and not only one of his boys took up his call, but all four did so. At the time of the funeral, all four of his sons were pastoring churches, and also one of his two daughters was in the ministry with her husband.

What about Uncle Sam's twelve children? Not even one of them was walking with the Lord. They had all rejected the religion of their father, and not one of them had turned to the Lord. Until his funeral, my father had been considered by many of his relatives as a spiritual failure, but as Hannah, the mother of Samuel declared in her prayer, "[God] raiseth up the poor out of the dust, and lifteth up the beggar from the dunghill, to set them among princes, and to make them inherit the throne of glory . . ." (1 Samuel 2:8).

If you are poor and needy, like a beggar on a dunghill, you can be sure that the Lord will hear your cry, and lift you out of your seemingly hopeless situation. He is looking for those who are poor in spirit. Jesus said that the poor in spirit would inherit the kingdom of heaven (Matthew 5:3). What does it mean to be poor in spirit? After the fall of Adam, every person who has ever lived has been born in sin, and will end in hell unless they turn to the Lord for His salvation.

In other words, our true spiritual condition is utter poverty; we are, in fact, *very* poor. But ironically, by nature we walk in pride, and most people feel that they are "not all that bad." When we finally see our great spiritual poverty, and when our attitude about ourselves lines up with our true condition, we will then be poor in spirit and not only poor in fact. It has been said that we all have great needs, but we are not all needy. When we become needy, God can do anything with us! He delights in raising the poor from the dunghill that their life is on.

CHAPTER 6

Our Soul Has Escaped as a Bird

On December 29, 2000 my wife and I left Guatemala to be in the U.S. for an extended time. We knew that the Lord was calling us to spend more time seeking Him and to write more books. One of the things that I packed to take to the U.S. was my journal where, since the 1960s, I have recorded some of the most important things that the Lord has done in our lives or spoken to us. I had never gone back to read most of it. But during the months before our move, I felt that the Lord was speaking to me to do so, because one of the best ways to see where we are headed is to see from where we have come.

My journal consists of a number of loose-leaf binders and many more pages in my computer. During the year prior to our departure from Guatemala, I had been reading from the first binder, a little at a time. I kept it on my office floor, next to the chair that I used mostly so that I would not forget to read from it. When I packed my personal things, I marked my place in that first binder and packed it along with the others.

When we arrived in the U.S., the Lord directed our steps in some very amazing ways to return to Dallas. This was not in our plans, but it turned out to be in *His* plans. We decided to rent an apartment, since there were not many good options for stand-alone houses. At that time, it was not easy to find apartments either, at least in reasonably safe neighborhoods. We finally found one, but it was on the third floor of a building without an elevator. One reason that we accepted it was that it had a fireplace, and we enjoy having a fire in the winter.

When we unpacked our things, I once again placed my journal on the floor of my new office, next to my chair. It was not until two months after we had rented the apartment that I finally picked up my journal and began to read where I had left off. The entry that I read next had been written almost 33 years before, at the time my wife and I were in Bible school.

I recorded there how I had gone to a classroom on campus to pray. It was not my usual place for my prayer time, but it was private and quiet on that particular day. As I prayed, a dove fell down into the chimney that was in that place and became trapped in a part of the fireplace. I heard it thrashing around and wanted to help it, but decided it was best to wait some time and allow it to tire so that after the dove exhausted its own efforts to free itself, it would be less likely to resist my help. Thus, my task would be easier.

My plan worked, and with little difficulty I was able to reach in and take hold of the dove. I then took it outside and set it free. I wrote in my journal the conclusions that I reached regarding this event and what I believed the Lord was showing me. One thing I realized was that when all our fleshly efforts have ended to free ourselves from our failures and what we are, He, in His mercy, will set us free from our captivity and bring us into His liberty. Only then will we be able to fly into the heavenly realm from where mankind fell in Eden.

Immediately after setting the dove free, someone entered the room. When I told that person what had happened, they were amazed that I just happened to be there at the very moment the dove fell down the chimney. In New York State, and other northern states in the U.S. the winters are very cold, and fireplaces are common in private dwellings. I grew up in such a house and though I had heard that birds can get trapped in chimneys, it never happened in our house. I have never even heard of it happening in the house of anyone I have ever known. What this person was saying was very true. I had just witnessed a very unusual event. If I had not gone there to pray, I would not have witnessed it.

Now, let's move forward 33 years to our apartment in Dallas where I was reading in my journal about the dove in the chimney. Literally *minutes* after reading this precise entry in my journal, and while I was still meditating on it, a dove fell down the chimney in our apartment and became trapped. It too was thrashing around. By the time I was able to reach it, it too was ready to accept my help. I took it outside and let it loose on the railing of our porch. To my great surprise, it walked around for a time. It seemed to have no fear whatsoever. Then it took flight, and I have never seen any bird express such happiness and joy by means of its flight. It was banking to the right and to the left, dipping and climbing. It looked like the happiest bird ever. For many days, it returned to our porch and would walk around on it and then take off again. It almost seemed to be coming back to thank me, or maybe it felt at home at our place!

During the weeks before moving to Dallas and for the two months after, the Spirit of the Lord kept bringing to my heart a Scripture. It was:

"My beloved spoke, and said to me: 'Rise up, my love, my fair one, and come away. For lo, the winter is past, the rain is over and gone. The flowers appear on the earth; the time of singing has come, and the voice of the *turtledove* is heard in our land. The fig tree puts forth her green figs, and the vines with the tender grapes give a good smell. Rise up, my love, my fair one, and *come away! O my dove*, in the clefts of the rock, in the secret places of the cliff, let me see your face, let me hear your voice; for your voice is sweet, and your face is lovely' " (Song of Solomon 2:10–14; NKJV).

Note that He is speaking here to His dove that abides in the clefts of the rock. He is the Rock. Those who abide in that Rock are His people. We see this confirmed in The Song of Solomon 5:2 where He comes to her dwelling and says to her, "Open to me, my sister, *my love, my dove,* my undefiled . . ." We see here that the Lord's dove is His Church (His Bride).

In the passage above, the Lord is calling His dove into a new freedom and liberty, and to a more intimate relationship with Him. My experience with the second dove was a clear confirmation that we had truly heard from the Lord regarding our move to the U.S. to spend more time seeking Him. Because of that experience, we knew that we were in the right place, at the right time, and doing the right thing.

He says to His love, "Rise up and come away." Why is He calling her to do this? He explains, "For lo, the winter is past, the rain is over and gone." The time of barrenness and death (winter) is past, and so are the storms and dreary days (rain). He is calling her to ascend into His heavenly liberty. I am confident that this awesome experience where the message of the dove's freedom was repeated to me after 33 years is not only for my wife and me. I am confident that this is a message of encouragement from the Lord, and that it is for all those who love the Lord in truth. Why am I confident that this message is actually from the Lord?

The prophet Isaiah tells us over and over that only the God of Israel knows the future (Isaiah 41:22–26; 46:9–10). Satan and his soothsayers do *not* know the future. If their "predictions" come true it is only because they know what is in the Bible or have heard the voice of the Spirit speaking through one or more of the Lord's servants.

I want you to consider with me just a few examples of God's foreknowledge in this experience. Who can deny His hand in this? Only He could have allowed another dove to be trapped in another chimney, 33 years after the first. Incredibly, this occurred precisely when I was reading about the first dove for the first time in 33 years!

To enumerate *all* the examples and evidences of God's involvement here would require too many pages of this book! I am actually giving here only a few of the many examples of His foreknowledge that surrounded this experience.

God's Foreknowledge Revealed

1. Only He knew, 33 years before the second experience, that He would cause me to once again set a dove free from its captivity in a chimney. Sadly, I have written about relatively few of my experiences in my journal, and I would not normally have written about such a seemingly insignificant experience. In retrospect, I can see that the Lord is the One who moved me to write about that first experience.

2. Only He knew, 33 years prior, that within minutes of reading my journal entry for the first time ever about the first dove, He would bring along the second dove.

3. Only He knew that we would rent an apartment in a complex that had only one place available—the third floor where we would have a chimney and fireplace. Incidentally, even before this second dove experience, we knew that God had chosen this particular apartment for us. The name of our ministry is Hebron, and after days of looking for an apartment in Dallas, the only suitable option was located on Hebron Parkway!

4. Only He knew that, while in Guatemala, I would read my journal only up to, but not including the experience of the first dove. He knew that I would then start reading about the first dove precisely at the time of the second dove!

5. Only He knew that I would not continue to read my journal again until we had already spent two months in the U.S.

and that then I would begin reading it at the very moment another dove would fall into our chimney. My entry about the first dove was on page 128 of my 236-page journal. I just happened to stop reading my journal in Guatemala on page 127, and then, months later, continued my reading on page 128, just minutes before the second dove arrived!

6. Only He knew that, for several weeks before this experience, I would be considering, almost daily, the truths about the dove being set free in The Song of Solomon 2:10–14.

7. He also knew that 33 years after the first dove, I would be asking Him if we were in the right place, doing the right thing. Before the experience of the second dove, I had spent many days wondering if we had somehow moved to a place that was not the Lord's perfect will for us. After the second dove, I had absolutely no further doubt!

Keep a Journal or Diary

Consider a couple other thoughts:

1. This shows how important it is for a person to keep a journal of his or her life. What if I had never kept one? My conscious memory did not recall my experience with the first dove until I had read about it in my journal. If I had not written about it in my journal, in my own handwriting, I would not have remembered it. In fact, I would not have even believed that this had occurred to me, especially as it related to the second dove.

2. As soon as I set the second dove free, a chorus came to me, taken from Psalm 124:7:"Our soul is escaped as a bird out of the snare of the fowlers: the snare is broken, and we are escaped." This is what the Lord will do for all those

who trust in Him. In these last days there will be greater examples of God's power to do this than at any other time in history, including the powerful protection of Israel when they were in Egypt, and the miracles He performed to deliver them.

It is definitely time to seek the Lord and forsake the call and attractions of this present evil world. I want to be included among the people that the prophet Daniel describes: ". . . the people that do know their God shall be strong, and do exploits" (Daniel 11:32).

CHAPTER 7

God's Great Kindness to a Repentant Father

"I was nothing but a womanizing drunk, and my wife had every right to divorce me and keep our children from me." Few people who end up in divorce are willing to recognize their guilt in the shipwreck of their marriage as Dr. Robert Morgan did with this unadulterated confession. Dr. Morgan is a retired physicist who worked in research for the United States Army. He gave me permission to tell his story in this book.

Dr. Morgan had two children with his first wife, a boy and a girl. After his divorce, he was not permitted to have contact with his children, and he never saw, nor heard from them again for almost fifty years, during which time he remarried. He had no idea what had happened to them. But God intervened in his life.

The way that the Lord used to reach his life with the Gospel is an example of God's sovereignty, but the end of the story is an example of God's love and mercy. God is waiting to have mercy on anyone who will turn to Him for help, confessing their sin and repenting.

The first book that I wrote was *The Final Victory: The Year 2000?*, published in 1991. It contains much more than a prediction about the timing of the last days. It contains many biblical secrets for understanding the last days and for rescuing us from private interpretations of Scripture. Therefore, when it was published, I believed that many people would be interested in discovering these truths. (Actually, we are probably selling more copies now, 28 years later, than we did then, precisely because of those important keys to understanding the last days.)

After the book was published, I decided to invest in a full-page advertisement in the best-known Christian magazine at that time. It was an enormous investment, but I felt that the sales would at least compensate the cost. To my amazement, we did not receive a single order from the advertisement. I was devastated, not only because no one seemed to be interested in my book, but because I felt like I had wasted a lot of the Lord's money on the advertisement.

Years later, Dr. Morgan contacted us and began to receive courses and books from our ministry. Later, when my wife and I were planning a trip near Dr. Morgan's home, at his invitation, we decided to pass by and spend some time with him and his wife, Jean. While there, we asked him how he had heard about us. He said, "Years ago, I received a copy of a Christian magazine that had an advertisement for your book. I clipped the ad, and kept it, thinking that I would order the book one day. After about six months, I finally got around to ordering it, and it changed my life and my wife's life. Since reading it, we have never been the same."

I then realized that the seemingly enormous investment had been worth it. "There is joy in the presence of the angels of God over one sinner that repenteth" (Luke 15:10). While I was lamenting the loss of the money that I had spent on the ad, the angels were rejoicing over two souls who had entered into the

Kingdom because of it![4]

Dr. Morgan and his wife continued to faithfully follow the Lord. He still had no idea about what had happened to his children. This brought him great sorrow and also a cry that God would intervene in some way. The Lord intervened and did something in his life that only an almighty God could do, and only a kind and merciful God *would* do.

Dr. Morgan's brother, Joe, lives in the area of Dallas, Texas. Joe has a married daughter who was in her mid-forties at the time of the following events. One day she called her father, Joe, and asked if he and her mother would be willing to accompany her to a real estate agent to look at a model home. At this point, I want to allow her mother, Sharon Morgan, to tell us what happened. She had wanted to find Dr. Morgan's children for 33 years. Here is her account:

> October 10, 2006 was an ordinary day. Joe and I had returned home the week before, from Tennessee, after a visit with Joe's brother Bob, his wife Jean, and other family members. Our daughter Sarah wanted to check out a model home as she and her husband were looking for a new home. We picked up Sarah and drove her over to a group of new home models about ten minutes from our home and, being a bit tired, we told her we would just wait in the car while she ran in. But she wanted us to look with her, so in we went. This was God at work, in His Infinite Wisdom!
>
> We were greeted by the real estate agent. Her name is Cindy Miles, and we chatted for a bit. Then we introduced ourselves: Sarah Monday, Sharon Morgan, and Joe Morgan. Later, Cindy told us that "a little bell rang in her head." She asked if Joe had any brothers. He said yes. She said, "Do you know Robert Morgan?" I don't know about anyone else, but now I had a really

---

4   Actually, hundreds more entered the Kingdom as a result of that advertisement, but those stories fall outside the scope of this book.

funny feeling. I was thinking, "We are in Texas; Bob is in Tennessee." So, I said to Cindy, "Where does he live?" And when she said Tennessee, I either shouted (or said in a whisper, I don't remember), "Oh my, you are our Cynthia!" And she said yes.

We all cried and immediately acknowledged God and His Glory. Joe's niece that he had not seen for almost 50 years, and who had been lost to us and our family was standing before us! Sarah's cousin! And how alike they were! We knew it immediately and their backgrounds were so similar. We all knew that this was definitely a "God Thing." Cindy called her mom, she also called her husband, and she called her brother Tim! We called Bob and Jean! Sarah called her husband Glenn.

We talked most of the afternoon and were overjoyed at being together! I had wanted to find Tim and Cynthia for about as long as I have been in the Morgan Family (33 years), but I had backed off. I felt it was not my place, yet I wanted us to be connected as family. How amazed we were at her close proximity to us and yet God chose the time and place for us to find one another! Cynthia said, "Well, God surely does have a great sense of humor!" How we agreed, for we could never have created such a scenario that God created for us. Joe and I might have stayed in the car, never discovering that Cynthia and Sarah, first cousins, were face-to-face! That the niece I longed to find was just inside.

It was decided that very day that we would *all* be going to Tennessee for a Thanksgiving celebration that would rival all others our family had shared. It was thrilling that Cindy and Tim were just as excited as we were! And just a few weeks later, we were all reunited and, best of all, Bob was reunited with his son and daughter after so many years! It was also quite special to watch him and his granddaughter, Ashley, become acquainted. What a day that was! And what grateful prayer and praise our

Lord heard from us that Thanksgiving. We had quite a gathering with all of us from Texas, in addition to Bob's son, Robert, his fun family of six, and Jean's daughter with her family of three. What a great time and such fun!

It was the prophet Isaiah who wrote: "For my thoughts are not your thoughts, neither are your ways my ways, saith the LORD. For as the heavens are higher than the earth, so are my ways higher than your ways, and my thoughts than your thoughts" (Isaiah 55:8–9). The Lord is telling us here, "If you figure a thousand ways to do a thing, I will do it a different way, and My way will be the best way."

How can we ever doubt His infinite wisdom, His timing, His ways? Our family is living proof of God's intervention in the affairs of men! At a time known only by the Lord, the Morgan Family grew. Cynthia and Sarah said, "We didn't just get another cousin, we just found each other!"

Postscript of February 15, 2011

There have been many times that two or more of us have been together since that day in 2006. We were thrilled to attend Ashley's college graduation. Other days were spent just hangin' out at the house with Cynthia. Just a few weeks ago, the Morgan Texas Contingency was in our home. What fun for Joe and me to share food and a great visit with Tim, his wife Sue, and daughter Ashley. With Cynthia (aka Cindy) and her husband Mike. With Sarah and her husband Glenn. We are so thankful that our family has grown and that we have grown so much in our relationships since that first gathering. And the closeness, the love that has blossomed, is again one of those miracles that God has blessed us with!

If there is even one person who doubts whether miracles don't or won't happen in their life, please let our family's miracle-story be proof that God does, indeed, grant miracles in our time. He alone knows what we do not know, and His ways are, indeed, not our ways. Just believe what is quoted by that prophet, Isaiah!

We are thankful for every day, every moment, that we now enjoy with the family that we did not have in our lives for those many years. Because now we *do* have one another! Thanks be to our loving God!

May both the believing and unbelieving reader consider the incredible number of events that were required for this story to have taken place, beginning with the publishing of *The Final Victory* in 1991. It is doubtful that Dr. Morgan's children would have wanted to see him if he had still been in the same spiritual condition as before. It is even more doubtful that God would have done this miracle for him if he had not turned to Him and prayed.

If even one key piece in this precious puzzle had been missing, the entire picture would have been lost. But the Almighty divinely orchestrated and organized each piece in a unique and essential sequence that only He was capable of doing. It is true that God could have done all of this in another way, but regardless of how He chose to do it, His handiwork would end up bringing Him glory. The fact is, He chose to do it as recorded above.

What if the book had not been published? What if the advertisement had not been placed? What if Dr. Morgan had not received a copy of that Christian magazine? What if he had not read it that month? What if he had not noticed the ad? What if he had not clipped the ad? What if he had lost the clipped ad? What if he had not ordered the book after all? What if his life and his wife's life had not been changed? What if Sarah

Monday and her husband had not been looking for a house? What if they had not checked with the real estate agency where Cindy worked? There are a multitude of options when it comes to a realtor. What if she had not asked her parents to go with her to the real estate agent? What if her parents had insisted on staying in the car? What if Cindy had not been working that day? What if she had not asked if they knew a Morgan in Tennessee? After all, Morgan is a common last name!

The "what ifs" could go on and on. For example, what about all the factors involved in leading Cindy to work in real estate, and then to work at that specific agency? Also, what about all the factors involved in Sarah Monday, Sharon Morgan's daughter, marrying a man who would continue to work in the Dallas area, and then end up wanting to buy a house in Dallas, and at that time?

Only those who choose to ignore God's hand in the lives of mankind can read a story like this and continue to reject the glory and reality of our God. Many, if not most, of those who have chosen to reject the knowledge and recognition of God have a vested interest in doing so—they want to be able to live their lives without accepting or acknowledging any of the restraints that their Creator might place upon them. In short, they want to live in sin and go their own way, and still be able to sleep at night, pretending that there will be no eternal consequences for rejecting God and for going their own way.

Unfortunately, pretending that God does not exist will not save anyone from the day when they will give Him an account of their lives. Believing a lie does not change the truth. If you have not yet done so already, it is time to open your heart to the Lord Jesus and ask Him to reveal Himself to you.

CHAPTER 8

The Prophetic Word Is Alive Today

The words of prophecy in the Bible often brought forth both resurrection life and also judgment and death. For those who know that God never changes, it will not seem strange that God's prophetic word still does the same today. In this chapter and those following, I want to share some examples of prophetic words that brought forth both life and death. In some cases, the prophetic word was fulfilled in ways that no man could have possibly contrived. The prophetic word brings forth life in some and death in others. The apostle Paul confirms this: "For we are unto God a sweet savour of Christ, in them that are saved, and in them that perish: To the one we are the savour of death unto death; and to the other the savour of life unto life" (2 Corinthians 2:15–16).

Life Is but a Vapor

"Come now, you who say, 'Today or tomorrow we will go to such and such a city, spend a year there, buy and sell, and make a profit'; whereas you do not know what will happen tomorrow. For what is your life? It is even a vapor that appears for a little time and then vanishes

away. Instead you ought to say, 'If the Lord wills, we shall live and do this or that'" (James 4:13–15 NKJV).

While I was a chemistry student at the University of Michigan, there were three other students who attended the same small church that I attended. We began to sing gospel music together, and we soon realized that it was no accident that our voices blended in a way that years of effort and practice could not have achieved. The main members of this quartet continued singing together and traveling in the United States for seven years.

Through a series of amazing events, we all independently decided to leave the university and become ministerial students in a well-respected Bible institute. We continued traveling on weekends and vacation time with the approval of the institute. The vision of each quartet member was that God's people are called to sing and minister praise and worship to Him. We realized that we are not called to minister to people with our music. Music in God's temple is for God. We are called to be priests unto God, and God's priests minister to *Him* (Revelation 1:6). The writer of Hebrews exhorts us: "By him therefore *let us offer the sacrifice of praise* **to God** *continually . . .*" (Hebrews 13:15a). Nowhere in the Bible do we find any godly sacrifice being offered to human beings or directed toward them for their pleasure and satisfaction.

As a result of our convictions, we became known as the quartet that would stand on the platform for 30 minutes and direct our worship and praise to God, forgetting about the people. Very often, during those times, God's presence would come on the people in such a way that they would simultaneously begin to worship the Lord along with us, without any invitation.

The importance of the concept of directing our words, prayer, praise, and attention to God instead of to the people cannot be overemphasized. Moses was a man like no other in history

(Deuteronomy 34:10). When Moses was 40 years of age, the Bible describes his heart and faith in Hebrews 11:24-27 this way: "By faith Moses, when he was come to years, refused to be called the son of Pharaoh's daughter; choosing rather to suffer affliction with the people of God, than to enjoy the pleasures of sin for a season; esteeming the reproach of Christ greater riches than the treasures in Egypt: for he had respect unto the recompence of the reward. By faith he forsook Egypt, not fearing the wrath of the king: for he endured, as seeing him who is invisible."

For the next 80 years, he was incredibly faithful to God. Yet, he made, what seems to many, one small mistake, and he was thereby disqualified from entering the inheritance that God had promised to His people. God told him to speak to the rock and that the rock would give forth his water (Numbers 20:8). Instead of speaking to the rock, he directed his attention to the people and spoke to them, and he smote the rock (Numbers 20:10–11).

Paul tells us that the Rock that was with Israel in the wilderness was Christ (1 Corinthians 10:4). God wanted to reveal through Moses one of the greatest secrets in the Christian life, and because Moses failed to reveal that secret, he was disqualified. By eliminating a man who was so holy, godly, faithful, and filled with glory, because of this seemingly small failure, God was showing to all ages the vital importance of this issue. If we direct our attention and ministry to the Rock, and speak and sing to the Rock instead of to the people, then the Rock will minister to the people and give them life-changing water. When we direct our ministry to the people (to the flesh), we disqualify ourselves from reaching the goal that God has for His people, and *He* will not minister to them. If the Rock does not minister to them, then what in the world can *we* accomplish through our own efforts?

Years ago, a godly woman was visiting our ministry for a week. Although she was experiencing God's presence, she was troubled by what she perceived to be an enormous difference between our way of worshipping and the way her own church worshipped. She kept asking the Lord to show her what the difference was. Near the end of the week, the Lord spoke to her and said, "Here they direct their worship to me. At your church they direct their worship to one another."

Getting back to the quartet, we all had this vision of ministering to the Rock instead of to the people, and the Lord was doing wonderful things through the group. However, after just one semester in the Bible institute, one member, whom I will call Bob, informed us that he was going to return to the university and finish his education.

Bob was unlike any other young man I have ever known. We had walked with him for a couple years by this time. When we first met him, he informed us that he would someday marry his high school sweetheart. He even told us that they had set the date for their wedding about six years in advance, and that he marked the countdown to his wedding day on his calendar daily. When we first met him, there were around 1,600 days left, or a little more than four years. From time to time, Bob showed us the calendar on which he daily recorded the new number.

The Prophetic Word Brings Death

To our great sorrow and dismay, Bob told us that he was going to return to the university, get his degree, marry on the predetermined date, join the army for four years, and then live happily ever after with his bride. We prayed with him, and the Lord gave a prophetic word of warning to him: if he did so, all his plans would be interrupted by his physical death. He ignored the warning and went on with his plans. He was definitely a man who planned ahead, but woe to any man whose plans are not the Lord's plans!

If we love the Lord and are called by Him, all things work for our good. For a moment it seemed like this was the end of the quartet. However, in the Lord's mercy, the young man that replaced him had an even better voice than Bob's. God wanted to continue propagating the message of the importance of ministering to Him instead of to the people.

Bob's plans proceeded like clockwork. He finished the university with fantastic grades. He married and joined the army. Because of his degree, he was able to become an officer, and he literally traveled the world for the army during the next four years. Four years later, having fulfilled his commitment to the military, he was discharged from the army. He boarded a commercial airline flight for his return home. In a few hours he would be with his wife, and they would begin the final phase of his plan—to live happily ever after. To this day, no one knows what happened to that commercial airline flight over India. The plane suddenly exploded in midair and all on board lost their lives. This was many years before international terrorism existed. Such a possibility was not even considered. The explosion was unexplainable, but the prophetic word had forewarned him of this end. Life is but a vapor, and when our plans are outside of God's perfect will, that vapor may very well be extinguished before its time and before our plans are fulfilled.

Man's plans fail, but God's word is always fulfilled, and He is still willing to speak to us just as He has spoken to mankind throughout history. Have you included God in your plans? Are you willing to ask Him what His plan is for you? Are you willing to listen for His voice and obey what He tells you? Only fools choose to ignore Him and His will for their lives! *His* plan is to bless you in *this* life and then throughout eternity!

The Prophetic Word Brings Life

My wife and I had the privilege of walking for many years with Brother Paul Stutzman, a man who was mightily used of God during a time of revival that touched the United States and the world. He was not used to bring that revival, but he became a well-known leader in one of its main centers in

Detroit, Michigan. It began between 1947 and 1948. It has been observed that 250 of the best-known ministries in the United States were raised up during those years when God was visiting His Church. Billy Graham's ministry really began between 1947 and 1949, the very years when that revival was fully under way. The ministries of people like Oral Roberts, T.L Osborn, Kathryn Kuhlman and many others began during this same period.

At the present time, there are many in the Body of Christ who call themselves prophets or apostles. Although Brother Stutzman never called himself a prophet, he was known in many circles in the Body of Christ for his accurate prophetic words that were given to people during the laying on of his hands. This is clearly a biblical practice. The apostle Paul wrote to Timothy saying, "Neglect not the gift that is in thee, which was given thee by prophecy, with the laying on of the hands of the presbytery" (1 Timothy 4:14).

Regarding his prophetic gift, Brother Stutzman had the reputation of never having given anyone a prophecy that did not come from God and that was not accurate. One of the marks of a true prophet is humility, and Brother Stutzman was a man who revealed that virtue. I never once heard him mention that reputation of himself, but many others gave that testimony about him.

In his later years, he was visiting a church where he had been invited to preach. After the service, the pastor of the church asked him to pray for a married couple in the congregation. Brother Stutzman did not know them since he had rarely, if ever, visited that particular church, nor did the pastor tell him anything about the couple. Everyone in the congregation knew that the couple had tried to have a child for many years, and after medical exams, they had been given no hope. The congregation also knew of Brother Stutzman's reputation.

As he laid his hands on them and began to pray prophetically, he began to speak about the new life that was in the womb of the woman. Many in the congregation gasped under their breath. They were sure that Brother Stutzman had just tarnished his reputation, because they knew that this sister could not have a baby. About a month later, that sister called her pastor and with great joy and excitement informed him that she was pregnant. Nine months later, she had her first child, and God was glorified once again by granting a life-giving prophetic word that revealed His life and His power.

The Prophetic Word Exposes Sin

During the revival that Brother Stutzman had been used in, one of the things that the Holy Spirit did was to reveal that God never changes. What He did in the days of old, He still does today. For example, the Lord showed that the prophetic word with the laying on of hands that the apostle Paul wrote about to Timothy is still available today. It was not something that God did only in the time of Paul and the other apostles. Brother Stutzman and others were used in ways that supernaturally convinced the honest hearts that God still speaks prophetic words to His people and also to individuals just as He spoke to Timothy.

However, during that revival, there were many skeptics, as there are today and always will be anytime that God visits His people. At the end of one of the meetings where Brother Stutzman was a leader, those who wanted prayer came to the front of the auditorium. They formed lines in front of a number of leaders, including Brother Stutzman. As he prayed for one person after another, a man finally reached him who was accompanied by four or five other men. His first words were, "Brother Stutzman, I do not believe in the laying on of hands with personal prophecies. I am a pastor, and I have come to this meeting with several of my leaders. I want them to see that there is no prophetic anointing here in spite of what we have heard. If you have a prophetic anointing, then tell me what my problems are."

At that moment, Brother Stutzman received a word from heaven, and he responded, "I do not know all of the problems that you have, but I do know that on the top of your list is adultery." To the surprise of his leaders, the man broke into tears and reached into a pocket and pulled out a literal list of his problems. He had come prepared! He showed the list to Brother Stutzman and also to his leaders. At the head of his list was the word "adultery." He confessed his problem before God and before his leaders. He left that service convinced that God still speaks prophetically! And sometimes He does so to reveal sin!

CHAPTER 9

Superterrorism Is Coming

"Return to the United States and give seminars in its cities about the superterrorism that is coming." The Lord spoke this to me in a very clear way in September of 1996 when my wife and I were living in Israel. When I heard this, I was in awe, shock, and with some serious concerns. In the first place, when we moved to Israel, we thought that we would be there until the Lord's return. When the Lord spoke to me, I knew that "return" meant to leave Israel on a long-term basis. This was going to be an enormous change of direction in our lives.

Furthermore, I could not imagine how we would organize seminars, at least not in English. We had spent many years ministering primarily to Latin American nations and Spanish-speaking people in the U.S. We had the necessary infrastructure to organize seminars in the U.S. among Latins, but I knew that the Lord was speaking to me about giving seminars in English to natural-born Americans. I had no idea about where to begin, but He did.

The Lord wasted no time in arranging everything for us. The very day that we got off the plane in the U.S. after leaving Israel, our U.S. secretary handed me a note. It had a man's name on it, and a phone number. She said, "This man wants you to call him." I had no idea who he was or why he would want to talk to me. I called him shortly after our arrival.

He immediately got to the point. He said that his ministry was involved in organizing seminars in many cities in the United States. He explained that he had read my book about the last days, and that he wanted to invite me to give a seminar in many cities. We agreed on the topic, and almost immediately I began to give seminars in 32 cities about the superterrorism that is coming to the U.S. The fool has said in his heart that there is no God, and only a fool could conclude that all of this was merely one coincidence after another. One thing is certain—superterrorism is coming to the U.S. and the terror of 9/11, four years after the seminars, was only the beginning!

What Did I Share in the Seminars?

As a young man, my initial career goal was to become a nuclear physicist. In my study of nuclear physics, I learned how to make a nuclear bomb. Making a bomb like the one dropped on Hiroshima is actually so simple that I fully appreciated why about half of the scientists who were involved in the Manhattan Project had doubts that the device would actually explode. The Manhattan Project was the codename for the collaboration of over 100,000 people who were involved in producing the first atomic bombs.

When the first atomic bomb was detonated in Alamogordo, New Mexico, the scientists who witnessed an incredible force, never seen before, stood in awe and fear. They were in awe, not only because the simple design actually worked, but because of the degree to which it worked. From the instant of detonation, the fireball formed within one millionth of a second, and reached a temperature of 100 million degrees centigrade.[5] Steel melts at around 1,400 degrees centigrade and boils at 2,870 degrees. At

---

5   See: "The Effects of Nuclear Weapons," atomicarchive.com, accessed June 13, 2019, www.atomicarchive.com/Effects/effects7.shtml.

100 million degrees of heat, everything that is touched by it is instantly vaporized, leaving a crater that is very deep and very wide.[6]

The scientists feared because, in that moment, they caught a glimpse of the horrific future that mankind faced if such power fell into the wrong hands. They feared also because their names would forever be linked to the team that unleashed the power of the worst weapon of destruction anyone could have imagined. Some of those scientists went to their graves feeling the weight of that responsibility on them.

What I shared in the seminars that I gave in 32 U.S. cities in the spring of 1997 was that the destructive power of nuclear weapons had, in fact, already fallen into the wrong hands. I explained that anyone with sufficient money and the desire to do so could build an atomic bomb, put it in a van, and park the van in long-term parking lots in any and all cities of the U.S. They could then detonate it remotely whenever they chose to do so. I explained that a single person or a small group of terrorists could destroy the U.S. without the help of anyone else. They could do so by building 100 bombs and then placing them in 100 vans, and then parking the vans in the 100 most important cities of the U.S., including Washington, D.C.

In case the terrorists had not considered this option, the July 12, 1993 international edition of *Newsweek* magazine clearly explained how to make the atomic bomb, complete with diagrams. The article also explained where it could be placed in New York City to do the most damage. They also informed everyone who wanted to build a bomb that a book for $23 would give them all the additional information they might need to do so.[7]

In the April 1997 edition of *Reader's Digest*, the world was also informed that the nuclear material needed to build a bomb

---

6   Ibid., http://www.atomicarchive.com/Effects/effects7.shtml.

7   Sharon Begley with Daniel Pedersen, Joshua Cooper Ramo, and Melinda Liu, "Chain Reaction," Newsweek, International Edition, July 12, 1993, 50–51.

was available on the black market for $200,000 per bomb. The article went into great detail about how the nuclear material was available on the black market.[8]

In the August 29, 1994 edition of *Time* magazine, there was an article entitled "Formula for Terror."[9] This article also explains how to make a nuclear bomb, along with diagrams. It also explains how much nuclear material is needed from the black market to make each bomb. The subtitle of the article is, "The former Soviet arsenal is leaking into the West, igniting fears of a new brand of nuclear terror." This article, along with the ones mentioned above, explain that there is very little security in Russia that protects weapons-grade nuclear material, and that it is very easy to steal it from there. The monthly wage of the guards is so low that almost any of them would sell bomb grade material for a small payoff. The U.S. keeps track of its nuclear material in increments of milligrams. Russia keeps track of it in increments of 55-gallon drums!

From the time that I learned how to build a nuclear bomb, in my heart I have both wept and laughed whenever government officials have talked about who has the bomb and who does not. The truth is that anyone who has the money and the desire to have the bomb can have it. The U.S. Federal government finally admitted that this is the case through the front-page article of *USA Today* on February 27, 2003. The title of the article at the very top of the page is "Fuel for nuclear weapons is more widely available than the public has been told."

The U.S. government exposed this six years after I explained this fact in the seminars. The main difference between what I said and what they said in their article is that they said that the terrorists could build a bomb and put it in a small pickup. I said that they could put it in a van, which of course would be much more concealed. The article explained that "now officials

---

8   Brian Eads, "A Shopping Mall for Nuclear Blackmailers," *Reader's Digest*, April 1997, 173–184.

9   Bruce Nelan, "Formula for Terror," *Time*, August 1994, 46-51.

believe the bad guys know the secret too." The secret is that a lot of bomb-making material is now available to terrorists, and bombs are quite easy to make.

In the March 13, 2003 edition of *USA Today*, on page 3A, this major article appeared: "Study: Nuclear stockpiles vulnerable." This was just two weeks after the front-page article of February 27, mentioned above, had warned the world. This last article explains that in Russia, security around nuclear stockpiles is very lax and easily breached, and that only 37% of their stockpiles actually have reliable security measures installed. In spite of this, the headline article of *USA Today*, about three years later on December 19, 2006, told how 600 pounds of weapons-grade nuclear material that had been "abandoned" by Russia in East Germany was shipped to Russia to be protected. The first question that comes to mind is whether or not the 600 pounds was all that was left of what had originally been abandoned? Could it be that terrorist organizations removed tons beforehand and just did not have a chance to pick up the last 600 pounds?

Another question is why the U.S. would have allowed that bomb-making material to be under Russian security when such security is almost non-existent? The man in charge of the operation to transfer it to Russia happily declared that securing it was "a Christmas present to the world." From what we know, it is more likely that it was a Christmas present to the terrorists!

A question that most readers would ask at this point is, "What are the terrorist organizations waiting for if they have nuclear bombs?" After all, it has been over 25 years since *Newsweek* told the world how to build the bomb and where to buy the material! Personally, I believe that there are two main reasons that the U.S. has not yet suffered nuclear attacks by our enemies.

First, God is a merciful God, and He rules in the affairs of man (Daniel 4:17). If we understand that the hairs of our head are numbered by the Lord, how much more should we realize that He controls every detail of life on earth! Nothing escapes Him, and nothing happens by chance. He has not lost control over His creation.

Second, those who want to take control of the U.S. must first have enough trained enemy combatants inside the country to make their move when the time comes. God will decide if and when that time comes. God is the sovereign King over all the earth, so we can be sure that the enemies of the U.S. will not be permitted to decide anything.

Some who are ignorant of a number of important facts have asked how God can be a God of love who has control over everything, and, at the same time, allows such horrible things like war, famine, violence, disease, etc. First, such a person probably rejects the historical account that the Bible presents. If the Bible is rejected, then we are all reduced to the confusion of innumerable opinions. An oft repeated axiom is that where there are two people, there are three opinions. Without the Bible, there is then no reliable basis for a discussion that will answer this question.

If we believe the Bible, then the answer is really quite simple. When Adam and Eve placed themselves under Satan's dominion of death, destruction, and darkness, all the horrible things that mankind has suffered ever since were part of the package. They came with the fall! Wars, famines, disease, accidents, and terrible events are all a result of Satan's influence. Satan is a liar, murderer, destroyer, and thief (John 8:44 and 10:10). How can we be so unjust as to blame these things on a loving God?

The question then becomes, "But why doesn't God just intervene and stop Satan from having any influence over mankind?" The answer to this question is also quite simple. God is looking for followers who truly love Him. He is looking for a wife, not a robot. A robot cannot give love. True love depends on a free will. Man is free to choose what Satan gives or else what

God gives. When God created Adam, He did not give him three choices—to either serve God, serve Satan, or serve himself. Adam was in a spiritual world that was enormously bigger and more powerful than he was. His options were to serve God or else serve Satan. God seeks people who serve Him out of love, not because they have no choice. By God allowing Satan to be in the world, mankind has a choice. People who choose Satan's ways, follow him as slaves, and are in bondage (John 8:34 and 44), but those who choose God's ways end up experiencing glorious liberty (Romans 8:21).

Some people think that they are serving themselves and that no one tells them what to do; they believe they do what they want. If they are honest with themselves, they will be forced to admit that there are things they do that they would prefer not doing. Maybe its smoking, or drinking, or drugs, or infidelity toward their mate, or lying, or stealing, or feeling hatred or jealousy. Maybe they have fears that they cannot conquer, or nervousness, or bad dreams, or sleepless nights. Maybe they are irresponsible in certain areas and go from one job to another. In addition, there are things that they *want* to do that they do not do. For whatever reason, they are incapable of doing those things. How blind they are to believe they do what they want! Without realizing it, they are under Satan's dominion if they are not under God's.

It is important to understand that God is also a God who establishes authority and boundaries, and He honors those boundaries Himself. This is true in both the natural and spiritual realms (Acts 17:26; Isaiah 10:13). He has declared that Satan is the "god of this world" (2 Corinthians 4:4). Why would He allow Satan to have influence in this world? Because to exercise our free will, we must have a choice, or we become robots. Do you want to love and serve God, or would you rather serve Satan and love his ways? Among other things, Satan's role in the earth gives us a choice about who we will serve.

Since the time of the fall of Adam and Eve, mankind has been under the kingdom of darkness ruled by Satan. That kingdom is filled with every evil and terrible thing imaginable, including wars, disease, violence, hunger, sorrows and failure. However, just as God recognizes the boundaries of Satan's kingdom, He also recognizes our free will. Satan has a right to rule over us as long as we are willing to live in his kingdom, but *we* have the right to cry out to God, and ask Him to deliver us from Satan's kingdom and allow us to live in *His* Kingdom. If we do so, Satan's rights over us are no longer valid, and we will have the testimony of the apostle Paul: "[God] hath delivered us from the power of darkness, and hath translated us into the kingdom of his dear Son . . ." (Colossians 1:13). God's door is open for those who want to live in the Kingdom of light instead of the kingdom of darkness. How foolish are those who blame God for the world's grave problems when Satan is the source of the slime and evil, and they knowingly or unknowingly choose to live in his evil kingdom! What kingdom do you want to live in? You make that decision every day. God's door is open to you right now, and you can ask God at this very moment to translate you into *His* Kingdom through the merits and sacrifice of the Lord Jesus Christ.

CHAPTER 10

Miracles of Provision Part 1

In January 1966, my wife and I moved from Ann Arbor, Michigan to upstate New York to attend a Bible training center to further prepare ourselves for the ministry. At that time, I was singing in a gospel quartet, and the entire quartet made the move also. We all studied during the week and then travelled to different churches on the weekends to sing and preach.

Initially, I assumed that we would have enough income from those trips to support us in the Bible school. However, I was gravely mistaken. We saw, firsthand, the condition of the leadership of some churches (but not all). As I already mentioned, our quartet had the reputation of standing on the platform for 30 minutes and just singing to the Lord. As King David shows us, the quartet realized that music is for the Lord, not to satisfy us personally or to minister to the flesh. David sang the Psalms to the Lord, not to entertain people (Psalm 30:4 is just one of over 25 Psalms that tell us we should sing to the Lord). As we sing to the Lord, the Lord draws near and meets with His people.

Many times we experienced wonderful visitations from heaven during our time in the churches. At the end of the services, the pastors would usually ask their congregations if they would like to bless the quartet with an offering, and help us with our travel expenses. The pastors usually assured the people that all that they gave would go to the quartet.

Some of the churches were quite large for those days, and we would all be encouraged when we would see that the people were giving generously. We all very much needed that financial help. Often, the offering plates would be filled with $20 bills, and sometimes there were *many* offering plates, each capable of holding 50 bills or more. Today, $20 is very little, but $20 in 1966 was equivalent to over $150 in 2019, according to inflation calculators. However, there were times when it was obvious to a casual observer that the congregation had given thousands of dollars even in the money of 1966. Our shock was understandable when the pastor would end up giving us a total of $200. From this type of repeated experience, we learned that some pastors were liars and thieves. How can anyone stand before a congregation and tell them that all that they give will be given to the group that was just used to bless them, and then keep almost all that was given for himself? Worse yet, how can such a person stand before God, and claim to be a pastor of His sheep?

I was the only married man in the quartet, so what I received had to be enough for two people. Counting the pianist, there were five of us, and so we would each receive $40 when a pastor would give us $200, and such an offering was quite common, regardless of what the people had given.

But God allowed questionable ministers to treat us this way for a purpose. Let's remember that He controls our circumstances. He wanted to reveal to us by experience that the One who fed the multitude with five loaves and two small fishes is still alive today. He wanted us to come to know the Provider and the Creator through personal experiences and encounters with Him.

He doesn't want our knowledge of God to be merely a doctrine that we hold in our heads. He wants us to experience the greatness of the God who declared that He never changes! He does not want to only change our mental beliefs. He wants to give us such wonderful encounters with Him that our hearts will be filled with a deep conviction of who and what He is, instead of only having a mental assent to His existence.

However, to experience the power of the One who sets the captive free, we must find ourselves in captivity. To experience the One who is our Provider, we will need to face some needs for which He alone can provide. To experience the One who heals the sick, we must face sickness. To experience the one who fights our battles, we must encounter some battles in our lives.

Through the prophet Jeremiah, God told His people to submit to the captivity of Nebuchadnezzar. The people of God in Jeremiah's day soundly rejected this message, and declared that Jeremiah was a traitor. That is pretty much the attitude of many Christians today. After all, why should we submit to captivity if all we need do is rebuke the devil and claim the victory?

But the Jewish people of that day did not understand one of the main reasons for their captivity. God explained through Jeremiah, "Like these good figs, so will I acknowledge them that are carried away captive of Judah, whom I have sent out of this place into the land of the Chaldeans *for their good* . . . And I will give them an heart to know me, that I am the LORD: and they shall be my people, and I will be their God: for they shall return unto me with their whole heart" (Jeremiah 24:5 and 7).

God was clearly assuring them that in their captivity they would come to know the Lord and would end up fully trusting in Him. These truths have not changed. Many Christians totally reject any captivity in their lives, and consider that suffering can only come to them if they have sinned. This is not the message of the Old Testament nor of the New Testament (for a few New Testament examples, see Acts 14:22; Romans 8:17; 1 Peter 4:1, 5:10; Philippians 1:29, 3:10).

The One Who Fed the Multitude Revealed Himself

My wife and I soon found ourselves in a captivity. We were low on food. Ever since we got married, 54 years ago, my wife has made homemade bread every week. But we were low on flour also and had no money to buy more. She looked into the flour canister and realized that there was not enough flour to make bread for the coming week. Then the Lord spoke to her to just dip it out with a cup. She knew that she should dip it out without looking into the canister. To her great joy, she dipped out enough to make bread for the following week.

I believe that the Lord put us into this captivity so that we would come to know Him as the One who can provide supernaturally. However, I believe that what He did in the following weeks would also be a testimony to the unbelievers. God knew that unbelievers, upon hearing about this experience, would assume that when my wife looked into the canister the first week, there was really more flour inside than she thought there was. So, the Lord had to make His miracle of provision even clearer. During the next week, He also chose not to provide money to buy flour. Once again, the Lord impressed my wife to just dip the flour out of the canister without looking in. Once again, she dipped out enough to bake bread for another week. We were at the scene of this event, and were not merely imagining that God was doing a miracle. We knew that we were experiencing a great miracle. Yet, God knew that some would *still* say that she had miscalculated about how much flour was in the canister the first time. So, He had to allow us to go through another week with no money. Once again, she dipped out the flour without looking inside, and out came enough to make bread for the third week.

Only a person who does not *want* to believe, or else assumes that I am lying, would discount this miracle, because when the canister was full, it had barely enough flour for three weeks' worth of bread. Remember, we had very little money and not an abundance of food. My wife has always been very frugal, but you can be sure that she was even more frugal during those days of scarcity, and she knew almost exactly where she stood with regard to how much flour she had. She knew that there was not enough flour for one week, much less three weeks!

A Different Captivity Came Next

For our second year in the Bible training center, I knew that I would need to get a job. Since my major had been chemistry, I was able to get a position in a laboratory belonging to the 3M Company. I was assigned the job of improving the formula of their photographic emulsion for the film they manufactured for portraits and printing purposes. It was a very respectable job, but I had to begin at the bottom of the pay scale for a new chemist. We knew that we would be unable to pay the tuition for our studies and the apartment that the school rented us, and at the same time buy food, clothing, gasoline for our car, and other necessities.

The Lord spoke to our hearts that He wanted us to use every penny I earned to first give our tithes to the Lord, and then pay our obligations to the school, and use what was needed for gasoline to travel to my job. We were not to use even one penny for food or personal needs. We obeyed, and the Lord did the rest. We never missed a meal because of not having food in our home.

Not one person on earth knew that we were living this way. For that second year of studies, my three brothers had also arrived at the school to prepare for the ministry. My older brother had been living in Massachusetts for some years, and my two younger brothers moved from Michigan to New York. Not even they ever knew that we had no money for food. Of course, they would have helped us in a heartbeat if they had known, but we would have become spiritual beggars, living off of the faith of others, and we would not have been submitting to the Lord's captivity. Once again, we came to know Jehovah Jireh, the Lord who provides, in a deeper and more meaningful way. We would not have traded for anything the joy of experiencing firsthand one miracle of provision after another, week after week for the entire year!

Our Previous Captivities Prepared Us for a Greater Miracle

During the summer of 1968, my wife and I offered to help start another Bible training center quite far from where we attended. When we arrived on the grounds that would become the campus of the new school, no one else lived there. There were a number of buildings, but the entire property had been totally abandoned for twenty years. There was no electricity and therefore no lights nor any appliances. There was no water except in a spring about 400 yards away from the buildings. There was no heat (and there were still cold nights when we arrived). We arrived there with two children. The oldest was a boy who was going on two, and the youngest was three months old.

We had a car that brought us to this isolated and forsaken place, but we had two other small problems. One was that the state registration for our car expired just after we arrived at this place, so we could not drive it. The second was that we had absolutely no money to renew the registration. However, that was not a very serious problem, because, since we had no money, we did not need the car. Driving a couple miles to the nearest store would have had no purpose anyway, since we did not have money to buy anything.

We had friends and relatives whom we could have called for a "loan" or an offering, but once again, my wife and I were not willing to become spiritual beggars. We tell absolutely no one when we have a financial need. Nor do we tell anyone that we are "living by faith." We realize that to say this to a person who has at least a little money is to basically have our hand outstretched, so to speak, with the desire to live by *their* faith rather than our own! So what happened?

We spent three months living at that place. It was basically like camping out, except that we had a roof over us, therefore, it did not rain on us. How did we eat for three months with absolutely no food? The God who provides revealed His mighty power and kindness once again. We definitely fasted more during those days than we normally did, and we did not eat three square meals every day. But He sent the ravens to us as He did for Elijah. The ravens were people who would come by to visit the future Bible training center. They were often very kind and good ravens who had no idea how much they were blessing us.

One man in particular came by the campus several times during those months. He was a Christian man who was the manager of the only grocery store in the area. We don't know why he would come by, but he would have in his car day-old donuts that he took from the store to give to his friends. Whenever he arrived, he would ask us if we would like some donuts. Of course, we never refused them! At that time, they were one of the most delicious meals that we could imagine!

At one point, my wife took the pennies from our little boy's piggy bank. It amounted to exactly 33 cents. At that time, some friends of ours were passing through the grounds of the future school, and my wife asked them if they would buy our son a box of dry cereal that he could eat without milk, and they obliged her. The cost of the box of cereal in those days was precisely 33 cents which literally amounted to our last cent! So, our little boy had food for a few days. We also ate wild berries that were growing in the enormous woods on the property. To this day, we do not know exactly how we survived for three months with no money and no food, but God provided, and we remained alive!

God can provide when there seems to be no provision. Our lack of flour prepared us to believe God for this greater captivity experience, but this experience also further prepared us for much greater financial captivities in the future that I will share in later chapters.

CHAPTER 11

Miracles of Provision Part 2

The experiences of financial captivity that we shared in the last chapter actually prepared us to trust God during times of far greater financial needs. When we learned to trust Him, we saw amazing miracles of provision that were beyond our expectation.

During our third and final year of the Bible training institute, I worked on the maintenance crew in the afternoons instead of continuing in a secular job. The maintenance supervisor knew that I enjoyed doing plumbing, so he gave me almost all the plumbing jobs during that year. It turned out that every type of plumbing work imaginable had to be done during those days, so I had a crash course in plumbing and learned to do basically any and all plumbing jobs.

The Master Plumber's Decision and the Lord's Decision

After leaving the institute, my wife and I, with our two small children, moved back to Michigan and stayed with my parents for a few days before we rented a house in a suburb of Detroit. I began looking for a job, and found an ad from a plumbing business that was looking for a plumber. I answered the ad, and the master plumber interviewed me from behind his desk. His first question was, "For how many years have you been a journeyman?" I asked, "What is a journeyman?" That question revealed my immense knowledge of the plumbing business, or rather my serious *lack* of knowledge! He explained that after four years of training under a master plumber, a person can take the required exams to get his license to be a journeyman plumber. He wanted to know how long ago I had gotten that license.

I had to admit that I did not have my license. He then asked me how many years of experience I had. My heart sank as I had to admit that, far from being a journeyman, I had a total of one year of experience! His response was, "No, no! I need someone who can go out and do any type of job imaginable, and afterward I will not get a call from the homeowner or business saying that they have a flood!" I explained to him that I could fulfill that expectation. I asked him to give me a ten-day trial period to prove to him that I could do it. To this day, I do not know what caused that master plumber to respond as he did to my request. He looked up at me from his desk and said, "Okay, I will give you a ten-day trial period."

At the end of the ten days, I returned to the plumbing shop late one afternoon, and as always, I gave him the keys to the service vehicle. He handed them back to me and said, "The trial period is over, and I have not had a single complaint. So, I am giving you the keys to the truck, and you can take calls during the evenings and nights, and you will make a lot more money." I was delighted that my family would have more provision.

He explained that when a call would come in, the hourly charge for my services would begin from the time I left my house, until I returned. In other words, the customer would have to pay a hefty wage for my travel time, as well as the time for the repair. Unfortunately, the first call came from an elderly couple who had just moved into a house that had a very small plumbing leak in the basement. They did not know the rules of the game. They lived a considerable distance from my house. I arrived, went to the basement, and fixed the leak in about ten minutes.

My heart was broken as I handed them a bill for the equivalent of $350 in 2019 purchasing power. This was the first time that I had been faced with charging people for my work. I drove home knowing that I could not continue to work as a plumber under those circumstances. I went into the shop the next morning and told the master plumber that I was quitting. He begged me to stay, but my decision was final.

As I drove home without a job, and as I considered all the money that I had been earning, I said to the Lord, "Lord, I know that I will never again earn so much money as I have been earning in this job, but I know that it is Your will for me to refuse to rob people in this way." The Lord must have been laughing, and I will explain why later. The truth is that we never make a sacrifice for the Lord or for righteousness that is not repaid many times over. I still had lessons to learn in this regard, but I would learn one more very soon.

Back to a Chemist's Wage

There have been times when a person can earn much more money by working with his hands than through a professional career. In those days, this was far more certain than it is in the year 2019, because millions of people have entered the U.S. who are willing to work for even less than the minimum wage. When my work as a plumber ended, I immediately sought for work as a chemist. I was hired by Firestone to work in one of its laboratories. Firestone is normally connected with the manufacturing of tires, but this factory produced different types of caulking, hot melt glues, and solvent cement glues. Some of the glues were used in the automobile industry.

Once again, I was hired at the beginning wage for a chemist. It was enough for my family to live on, but with very little left over at the end of the month. The Lord blessed me in ways that were supernatural, enabling me to develop products that saved the company a lot of money. I knew for a certainty that my knowledge of chemistry was not the reason for my success, but rather that God caused me to discover things that were truly surprising both to me and to other chemists. So much so, that one chemist who worked in the laboratory I had been assigned to, when he saw what was happening, decided to quit his job and go back to the university to study more chemistry. He was certain that more study would cause him to make the same type of discoveries. He didn't know my secret source—God!

After a little more than six months with Firestone, I believed that God was speaking to me about working with my hands once again, but in a legitimate business. I wasn't certain that I was hearing God's voice, so I asked Him to cause the management of Firestone to make the decision for me. How would they do that? In light of what God had done through my research working as a chemist for them, I knew that it was time to ask for and receive a significant raise in my salary. I knew more or less what the other chemists were making.

I talked to my immediate boss, and I asked him for a raise up to a specific amount. It was a raise of 50 percent more than what I had been making. He said that normally Firestone would only approve a raise of 10 percent at a time, but he felt that he could obtain that raise for me because of two factors. First, their plant was having a hard time keeping chemists on a long-term basis, and second, just by chance, the vice president of Firestone was going to visit our plant the following week. He said he would talk to him directly about me, and that he was certain he would approve the raise.

I knew that he was not a believer, and that he would therefore not understand that I was asking God to choose my future by means of the decision of the management of Firestone. Therefore, in order to not go into detail regarding what was happening in my heart, I simply told him that I was a spiritually minded man, and that for me, whether or not I received that precise amount of raise would determine my future with Firestone. I explained that if the raise was for one dollar less per month, that I would give him my two weeks' notice and would be leaving Firestone.

Between a week and 10 days later he called me to his office. When I entered he was very excited as he exclaimed, "They approved the raise!" He told me how much the raise was for. It was for only a few dollars less than I had asked for. I then proceeded to remind him of what I had told him before, and that I was therefore giving him, at that moment, my two weeks' notice and I would be leaving Firestone. He began to plead with me not to leave. He said, "You don't understand what we are going to offer you. You'll be the head chemist of one of our labs here. Once you have that title, you will be able to go anywhere, and they will hire you in a moment." I don't recall what I answered him, but I felt almost as badly as he did, as I explained that my decision was final.

After resigning from Firestone, my new job consisted in helping a friend install aluminum rain gutters on houses. My friend subcontracted jobs from contractors in the Detroit, Michigan area. He had very little work, and during the following month of February, I made a total of seven dollars. Even so, my wife and I were both at peace and knew that the Lord had chosen for us.

Around June of that year, my friend informed me that he was leaving the U.S. soon to go as a missionary to the Philippines. He asked me if I wanted to buy his business. It basically consisted of a pickup truck that was 10 or 15 years old, and a few hand tools. I assured him that I was willing to buy it. At that time, because of my friend's lack of jobs, I was still making about the same that I made as a chemist.

My friend didn't tell me when he would be leaving, but one morning in the month of July, as we began working, he informed me that at noon that day the business would be mine. I said that would be fine, and precisely at noon he told me goodbye. Only God could have ordained and orchestrated what happened one hour later. A contractor in Detroit called me on the phone and asked me to meet him at a certain address. It was very easy to give him my time, because there were no other jobs on the horizon.

When I arrived at the address, the contractor was waiting for me. His words to me were beyond belief. He said, "Do you see this house? Put gutters on it as fast as you can. And when you finish, put gutters on the next house as fast as you can, and then on the next house and the next. Put gutters on every house on both sides of this city block."

From that day on, for the next two years, my helpers and I usually worked from morning until night. One job after another came in. In the first year that I had the business, my clear profit was the equivalent of $300,000 in 2019 purchasing power. Before selling the business to my brothers, during my second year, I was making $600,000 a year. Imagine! Not long before, I had told the Lord that I would never again make as much money as I was making as a plumber. I am quite sure that the master plumber himself who had hired me was not making that amount of money. This is why I mentioned above that the Lord must have been laughing when I told him that I would never again make as much money! Doing God's will never ends up being a sacrifice. He always returns to us, blessed and multiplied, any *seeming* sacrifice that we might make. Also, my wife and I knew that the riches of the Lord, and the privilege of doing His will and responding to His call are far greater riches than anything this world can offer.

Be Careful and Obedient When God Sends Blessing

Throughout history, almost without exception, whenever God has blessed a person or a nation, that person or nation very quickly forgets God and chooses to live for the flesh and in accordance with their own opinions. The man who wrote

Proverbs 30:8–9 understood the danger when blessing comes. He asked the Lord, ". . . give me neither poverty nor riches; feed me with food convenient for me: Lest I be full, and deny thee, and say, Who is the LORD?"

Israel had no sooner entered the Promised Land, when the entire tribe of Benjamin chose to go to war to protect the men of Gibeah who had become homosexuals and killed a man's concubine by rape (Judges 19:22–28). We know that this occurred during the very first years that Israel was in the land, because Phinehas was the high priest, and he had been an adult during Israel's forty-year journey from Egypt (compare Numbers 25:6–8 and Judges 20:28).

The United States is a modern example. The economy of the nation was prospered enormously after the end of WW II. Only seventeen years later, the Supreme Court removed prayer and the Bible from public schools (in 1962 and 1963). Then, in 1973, the Supreme Court ruled that abortion was a constitutional right. Since that ruling to the date of this writing, approximately 60 million babies have been killed in the U.S. The fruit of these decisions is evident when a person considers the graphs of the yearly rates involving murder, robbery, assault, divorce, poverty, and other tragedies of life. The numbers on those graphs were quite constant and very low until 1962. From then until now, all those numbers have increased exponentially.

Now, homosexuals can be legally married, and young children who "identify" with the opposite sex can use the bathrooms, locker rooms, and showers of the sex that they consider themselves to be instead of the sex they were born as. Also, many universities have co-ed dormitories where a girl might find herself with a boy as her roommate. We could say that our leaders have lost their minds, but the truth is that if we refuse to serve the God of Creation, the only other option is to serve the god of this world with all his wicked perverseness. If we reject light, the only other option is darkness. If we reject life, we can only expect death.

No sooner had my wife and I begun to experience a tremendous level of prosperity, when the Lord began to work in our lives to teach us some important lessons about handling prosperity. As I already mentioned, when we bought the business from my friend, it included a very old pickup that had holes from rust in its body. About then, the engine of our used car, which we had recently purchased from an elderly neighbor, suffered a premature and fatal death. By then, we had enough money to buy a new car with cash. But the Lord spoke to us to use the pickup as our family transportation, as well as for work. So, we drove it to church and back every Sunday, along with all the ladders, gutter supplies, and sometimes old gutters loaded on it.

The members of our church, as well as the pastor, loved new, big, and expensive cars. I am not sure who was humbled more—my wife and me, as we drove the old clunker, or the members of the church who had to endure the embarrassment of the world seeing that a very poor family attended their church!

Just Enough to Do God's Will

During the last three months that I owned the business, my wife and I calculated the total amount of profit we would need to receive each week to meet all our needs. Seven years earlier, we had received a call from the Lord to go the Philippines as missionaries. In addition to our current financial obligations, we needed to have the money required to build a house in the Philippines. We also needed to buy some very important essentials for living in the Philippines. For example, we would need a generator that would provide our own source of electricity. We would need a kerosene refrigerator, a washing machine, and many other very expensive items. In addition, we would need to purchase the transportation to the Philippines for a family of six, to say nothing of the cost of shipping all of the very heavy equipment.

Calculated in 2019 purchasing power, we needed $12,000 of profit every week for three months. The Lord faithfully provided that amount, and little did we know how precise our calculation would prove to be. That amount was just enough to do the Lord's will. When we arrived in the Philippines, we had a total of $3 (or $18 in 2019 purchasing power) left, but we were on our way to live in the jungles of the Philippines, so it was not a problem. However, what we experienced on our way to the Philippines provided many more examples of divine intervention and divine provision. The next chapter tells a little of that story.

CHAPTER 12

The God Who Provides without Provision

Six months before moving my family to the Philippines, I went there alone for a month to accomplish two things. The first was to begin construction on our home. The second was to acquire the services of a man in Manila who knew how to obtain the visas we would need. We would need to live in the Philippines with work permits, rather than arriving as tourists. The man whom we chose for this task was recommended by Brother Paul Stutzman, who founded the Bible school where I would be teaching. Brother Paul assured me that this man was very responsible, and that he could obtain our visas within one month. We would soon discover it was not to be.

One month after returning to the U.S. and continuing with my business, I received a message from Brother Paul. He said that the visas had not yet been obtained, but that they would be ready within another month. About one month later, I received a similar message from our brother. As each month passed, I received several similar messages, until finally, a week or so before it was time to fly to Oakland, California, I received a message that our visas would be waiting for us in the Philippine Consulate in California. We had tickets for a cruise ship that would be departing from Oakland. We chose this means of travel since it was, by far, the cheapest way to travel to the Philippines with our enormous amount of cargo. Well in advance of our departure date, we shipped the largest and heaviest pieces of our cargo by freight to the Oakland pier where it would be loaded onto the ship.

We confidently boarded our flight to Oakland with our four small children who were between the ages of three months and five years. The stewardesses of the airline decided to put us in first class seats with our small children. They probably felt compassion for the mother and her little ones. Then, upon arriving, just as confidently, we went to the Philippine Consulate to pick up our visas. When I told the agent that I was there to pick up our visas, she asked me for my name. She then began to search through her files, and to my utter shock, she informed me that no visas had arrived for us.

With some very deep concerns in our hearts, my wife and I returned with our children to the missionary guesthouse where we were staying. Our deep concerns got even deeper after calling the man in Manila who had promised me that our visas would be ready within the first month. When he answered his phone, I told him who I was, and asked him where our visas were. His response was short, to the point, and very agitated. He said, "Don't ask me that question," and he hung up on me as though I had been calling him from the other side of the street.

We had known enormous prosperity for some time, but we had kept back just enough money to reach the Philippines with our four small children and move into our new home. We did not have enough money to fly back to Michigan, and spend time there, before returning to California. Besides, we would not only lose the money we had paid for our tickets on the cruise ship if we did not board the ship, but it might have taken weeks or months to find another option for traveling to the Philippines. Also, what about the heavy cargo that was already on the ship? We knew that it was time to pray and to hear from heaven regarding the next step.

Take Up Your Cross and Follow Me

As we prayed, the Lord spoke to me two simple instructions. He said, "Take up your cross and follow Me." I knew that He was saying that we should board the ship and move forward in His plan for us. He then gave me the answer regarding how to board the ship without the Philippine visas. As international travelers know, no airline or cruise ship will allow a person to board a plane or ship if the person does not have a valid visa for the country of destination, if that country requires a visa. Furthermore, to enter a country as a tourist with the idea of obtaining a work visa afterward is almost never approved, except maybe in the United States! So, that was not an option for us regarding the Philippines. The Lord instructed us to go to the Japanese Embassy and obtain tourist visas. With those visas, we would be allowed to board the ship, since a stop in Tokyo was part of the ship's itinerary, and we could disembark there if we still did not have our visas for the Philippines.

In the small missionary guesthouse where we were lodging in California, the guests ate together at a large table. Among the guests who were lodging there, was a group of three women who had been missionaries in the Philippines with the same organization for 15 years. They were returning for their fourth five-year term. Three months earlier, they had been told that their visas had been approved, and that they could arrive in Oakland to pick them up and then fly on to the Philippines. However, they had spent three months living in the guesthouse, waiting for their visas to actually arrive to the Philippine Consulate.

When they heard from us that we were going to board our ship, and trust in the Lord to work things out, they asked us if we had an organization in the Philippines that was working on obtaining our visas. We told them that we did not have anyone working on our visas. They counseled us to not even consider boarding the ship. They explained that their organization had a team of people in the Philippines who had been working on obtaining their visas for eight hours every day for three months, and that they still had not gotten them, and this after already having spent 15 years in the country. They were very convincing, but we were convinced that the Lord had spoken to us.

A Confirmation of God's Will

At breakfast time each morning, one of the guests would be asked to read a short passage of Scripture that was a continuation of where their reading had ended the previous morning. The next morning, on the day of our embarkation, the manager of the home asked me to read the next passage. One of the few verses included in the reading was this verse: "And blessed is she that believed: for there shall be a performance of those things which were told her from the Lord" (Luke 1:45). Everyone at the table knew about our situation and our decision to board the ship. They almost spoke in unison, saying that the fact that this was in the short passage that came up for that morning, and that I was chosen to read it, surely indicated that we were obeying the Lord.

We boarded the ship, and our journey began. The trip from California to the Philippines was to be divided up into three weeks. After the first week, we were to arrive in Hawaii. The second week would end in Tokyo, Japan and the third week in Manila, Philippines. We were ending our first week when we received a telex message. A telex was a legal method of communicating long before the world discovered email. The message was from the Philippine Embassy in Tokyo, letting us know that our visas were waiting for us in the Embassy there. To say the least, we were delighted, greatly relieved, and encouraged that the Lord had indeed intervened on our behalf. Some might conclude that the man in the Philippines pulled some strings and got our visas sent to Tokyo. However, he had no clue that we were even boarding a ship that would pass through Tokyo.

Remember, he hung up on me before I could even explain to him our predicament and itinerary. He did not know where we were or where we were going at the time. It was God who pulled the strings from heaven! To this day, we have no idea of why anyone would have sent our visas to Tokyo!

We joyfully sent a response back to the Philippine Embassy saying that our ship would arrive in Tokyo on Saturday morning and that we would go directly to the Embassy. They telexed back saying that the Embassy was closed on Saturday. I telexed back, pleading that someone would do us the favor of working overtime, since our ship would be there for only 12 hours. The final telex came back, saying that they would receive us on that following Monday. End of story!

We realized that we would have to disembark. A few days later, we found out more details about the cruise line with which we had booked our reservation. We learned that it had two sister ships, and that they were both 25 years old, and that they were both taking their last trip as cruise ships. They were both going around the world on a three-month cruise, and after that trip, they would both be converted to cargo ships. It turned out that the sister ship was coming behind us and that it was making all the same stops just ten days later. Of course, we also knew that, even if the company were willing to allow us to change ships ten days later, it would be almost impossible to get a cabin on the other ship. We already knew that our ship had been totally booked months before, and that the sister ship had been totally booked also.

With great trepidation, we contacted the cruise line and asked if it would be possible to change our reservation to the other ship. Of course, they knew, as we did, how unlikely that would be. However, to their surprise and ours, there were actually two cabins that were not occupied on the sister ship—two and no more—along with two important details that only God could have worked out. First, the two cabins were next to each other, and second, they were connected by an adjoining door! To our great surprise and joy, the cruise company said that they would give us *both* cabins at no extra charge. Problem solved! God is good!

Who could be so foolish as to attribute all this to just good luck? Imagine, both ships were completely full, but there just happened to be two empty cabins on the second ship with its thousands of passengers, *and* they just happened to be right next to each other, *and* they just happened to be connected by a door. God was looking out for the four little children who were called to endure all this with their parents. Even though there are very few connected cabins on cruise ships God found two on the sister ship and saved them for six very needy people who would be moving from one cabin to two cabins!

A City for the Wealthy

On our ship there were 21 other missionary couples who were going to different countries. We became friends with one couple who was returning to Japan as missionaries. They gave us the sobering news that Tokyo was the most expensive city on earth (at least, at that time, and at this writing it is still one of the top ten most expensive cities). They did not believe it would be possible to stay in Tokyo for less than $300 a day ($1,800 in the dollars of 2019), counting a hotel and three meals for five people. Our 3-month old infant was nursing. (Here and in the rest of this chapter I will refer to the dollars of that time.)

We knew that we had an enormous problem, because the total amount of money that we had at that time was $300, and we had to spend 10 days in Tokyo, waiting for the arrival of the sister ship. But God never has a problem. Yes, we had brothers who would have sent us as much money as we would have needed, but, once again, we have never been willing to become spiritual beggars, asking others for financial help.

As we were nearing the Tokyo port, the Lord spoke to me that we had learned to trust in His provision. When we needed financial provision, we would come to Him and present our need to Him. He would then give us the money that we needed, and we would then trust in that money until it had been spent, and we would then go back to the Lord and request more. He said that we had learned to trust in His provision, but that now He wanted to teach us to trust in the Provider, who can provide *without* provision. We did not know how He would miraculously provide without provision, but we were soon to find out how.

We fully realized that upon disembarking we would have to take all our belongings off the ship and store them with a special company called a Marine Terminal. They safely store people's belongings in a port for short periods of time—of course, for a hefty price! Our belongings not only included ten suitcases that we had in our very small cabin, but also ten other very large pieces that were in the ship's cargo hold. Those pieces included a diesel generator and a large and heavy refrigerator that worked by burning kerosene. I would never have believed that a fire could be used to produce ice, but it actually works. We also had a washing machine and other large wooden crates along with two 55-gallon drums.

As soon as we disembarked, we went straight to the office of the Marine Terminal, and committed our ten suitcases to their care. We had already instructed the purser on the ship that we would need them to unload all of our cargo onto the pier. He said it would be on the pier within 30 minutes. The Marine Terminal collects the payments in advance, and they presented us with a bill of $60 to store the 10 suitcases for 10 days. That took a large part of our $300! Our hearts sank when we realized that there was no way that we had enough money to store the ten large pieces of cargo with them. The suitcases were nothing compared to the other pieces, neither in size nor weight!

Apparently, All Was Lost

We went back to our ship and looked on the pier for our things. They were not there, even though 30 minutes had elapsed. We entered the ship and asked the purser if he knew what was happening. He assured us that everything would be off the ship very soon. We waited for about another 30 minutes, and then approached the purser again. He then asked me several questions. One was if our things had arrived at the pier in Oakland, California at least two weeks before the ship departed? I assured him that everything arrived well before that. He then said to me, "Sir, I do not know where your things are. Either they did not arrive at the pier soon enough or else they were stolen, but I can assure you of one thing. Your cargo is *not* on this ship!" I knew that they spray painted large numbers on each piece of cargo that they put into the ship's hold. It was obvious that anyone could have seen our ten different numbers, especially the ship's porters who loaded and unloaded the ship trip after trip. We concluded that we would be arriving to the Philippines without any of our most important belongings.

Before we departed from the missionary guesthouse in Oakland, someone had given us the phone number of a missionary guesthouse in Tokyo. When it was given to us, we did not realize that it was a divinely appointed contact. We called the number and asked if they had room available for us. The man asked who we were and how many of us there were. As soon as he heard the details, he said emphatically, "No, I am sorry but all of our rooms are taken." I began to pray earnestly in my heart but not with my mouth. In a few seconds, he said, "Let me ask my wife just in case she can make an arrangement." I knew that our only other option would be a hotel that would cost far more than we could pay, and we did not have credit cards in those days. I also knew that the cost of ten nights in the guesthouse was far more than we could pay, but the Lord had said he would provide without provision. A few minutes later, the man came back on the phone and told me that we could stay with them.

This Is to Know Me

Upon arriving at the guesthouse and checking in, Barbara took our children up to the room where we would be staying while I worked on taking care of the luggage. She later expressed that she was beyond being overwhelmed with our situation. For the first time in our lives we were in a foreign country, and few people spoke English. We were almost penniless, and had to stay there for 10 days. We had just gotten the news that all of our main cargo had been lost. We were with four very small children, facing all that caring for children entails, especially for a mother, and, for the first time in our married lives, we had no way to pay our expenses!

At least three of the children were old enough to know that things were not going so well. In fact, when we were walking on a street in Tokyo, our four-year-old daughter was greatly impacted by what she saw and heard. Upon hearing the speech of the Japanese and seeing how differently they looked from Americans, the confusion and conflict in her little heart was revealed by her words. Looking up at her mother, and in a pitiful tone of voice she said, "We are a *long* way from home, aren't we mommy?"

Since Bible school days, a longing in Barbara's heart was to know the Lord in an ever deeper way. Paul's longing in Philippians 3:10 had become her longing—". . . that I might know Him . . ." Later, Barbara told me that upon entering our room with the children, and feeling devastated, she heard what seemed to be the audible voice of the Lord. It was something that she has experienced only three times in her entire life, and this was the first time. His voice said to her, "This is to know me." Once again in our lives, we were submitting to a captivity, like that to which Jeremiah had told Israel to submit. We were about to know Him in ways that we had never experienced before.

During our ten days in the guesthouse, the staff grew very fond of our children. Also, I was able to help them with a few little things that needed to be fixed. At the end of the ten days, I went into the office to pay our bill, knowing full well that I did not have enough money to pay what we owed. No one in the home had the slightest idea about our financial situation. As I stood in front of the manager's desk, he tallied up the charges. When he finished, and wrote down a number that was far beyond my means, he stopped, and looked up at me and said, "You know what? I am going to give you the nightly rate that we give to our own missionaries." He then presented me with the new total bill. Out of the $240 that we had left, the new total left me with just enough to give the cabin attendant on the sister ship the recommended tip of $30, and leave us with $3 when we arrived in Manila. Fortunately, someone was planning on meeting us there.

It wasn't until some years later that I realized the enormity of the miracle the Lord had done in that man's heart. Since our time in Tokyo, and throughout the years, we have stayed in many missionary guesthouses, and never once did any house *ever* give us a discount. In fact, we learned that that man was risking his position by giving us the nightly rate that only their missionaries were charged.

While we were in Tokyo, the husband of the missionary couple with whom we became friends on the voyage, invited me to accompany him on some errands he needed to do in Tokyo. As we went from store to store, he would look in the store windows and tell me that he was planning on buying one expensive item after another that were on display. It became clear that he had an enormous amount of finances. As we passed a camera shop, he pointed out a $500 camera in the window and said, "I am going to buy that later today." Our poverty became more and more evident to me, though he had no idea about our financial situation.

As I was feeling a little heavy in front of the camera shop, the Lord asked me, "If you had a million dollars, would you buy that camera if it were not My will for you to buy it?" I responded, "No, Lord, I would not buy it." He then asked, "If I wanted you to have it, do you not believe that I could provide you with the money to buy it?" My very sure answer was, "Yes, Lord!" He said, "So what is your problem?" That brought a deep peace to my heart, and what my friend told me a few minutes later did not affect me at all. He said that he would have to leave me because he had an appointment to pick up his new car from the dealership. The Lord had told me that He would provide without provision, so my heart was at peace.

All Is *Not* Lost!

We finally boarded the sister ship with great joy, although our hearts were also heavy because we had lost most of our important things. About one day before we arrived in Manila, we received another telex. It said that they had found all of our things, and that they had, in fact, been on the first ship, and that they were storing them for us on the pier in Manila, free of charge! The Provider had indeed provided without provision! In this case, the Lord must have blinded the men who searched for the ten large numbers on the sides of ten large pieces of cargo. All these details are further examples of the many infallible proofs of God's reality, and of His resurrection. He is still alive! He can do for you anything you need Him to do if you will only give Him an opportunity to come into your life in a greater way or maybe for the first time.

CHAPTER 13

God Plans Our Trips and Provides for Them

Would You Happen to Know Someone?

After we had been teaching in the Philippines for two years, we felt that the Lord spoke to us to return to the U.S. during the three months when there would be no Bible school classes. The only problem that we faced was that we had a sum total of $600 to our name. As missionaries, only $85 a month had been promised to us as support. Of course, we had very few expenses, but to save $600 in two years on that very small income was almost miraculous. That was just the right amount to travel from the Bible school on our distant island to Manila. Flights to the U.S. depart only from there.

The nation of the Philippines consists of over 7,500 islands, of which about 2,000 are inhabited. The total distance between these islands is over 1,100 miles. The distance between the airport on our island and Manila was almost 500 miles, so of course, this trip required six airline tickets for our family. We realized that, after our flight to Manila, we would have just enough money to pay for a few days' lodging in the missionary guesthouse that we had come to know.

We arrived safely in Manila, and checked into the guest-house. Most surely, getting to Manila was the easy part, financially speaking. The hard part was how to buy six tickets to fly from Manila to Detroit, Michigan, since we had absolutely no money to buy them. This guesthouse was larger than the one we stayed at in California, and not everyone ate their meals at one large table. There were many smaller tables, and the manager assigned everyone to a different table for each meal. This way, the missionaries got to know one another.

For our first meal, we were assigned to a table to which only one other person had been assigned. She was an older lady, and as we were eating and getting to know each other, she asked us a question that we had a hard time believing we were hearing. She asked, "Would you folks happen to know two adults who would like airline tickets to the U.S.? The reason is that I am travelling to the U.S. with ten orphans who have been adopted, and I need two people to help me, and who will be responsible for a couple of them during the journey."

We told her that we just happened to know two such adults, and that we were the adults, and would be very happy to help her, which we did without the slightest problem at any time during the trip.

I would ask the reader, "How many times have you met a complete stranger who within a few minutes offered you a couple of airline tickets that were worth thousands of dollars, and that just happened to be the precise tickets that you needed at the moment? It never happened to us before or after this experience. What are the chances of us being assigned to that particular table with that particular person who had that particular need, when we had just arrived in Manila and were wondering how God would provide the airfares for our trip?

Remember, the Lord had spoken to us that we were to return to the U.S. for the summer months, at a time when we had just enough money to go no further than Manila. Now, this lady just happened to be assigned to a table where we had a very particular need that could meet her very particular need. Some might say that all this was sheer coincidence, but this book presents simply too many "sheer coincidences" for any honest person to not see the hand of God in them. Remember, also, that it was God who told us to return to the U.S., and it was God who miraculously and quickly provided the tickets to do so, when there was no natural hope of that happening!

Within a few hours from the time that we had the provision for two tickets to the U.S., I received a phone call from the U.S. During our years in the Philippines, we probably received at most three phone calls. There was no phone service where our home was. It was my brother calling, and he told me that he had made a deposit into our account for a sizeable sum. He did not know of our plan to return to the U.S. for the summer, and so he could never have known that what he had given us was precisely what we needed for the children's tickets! Our God is wonderful and amazing!

For God, There Is No Difference Between $2,000 and $20

I worked for most of the summer for my brother in the business I had sold to him and to my other brothers. In the meantime, he had bought the other two brothers out. He paid me very well during the months that I worked for him, and by the end of the three months, we had managed to save $2,000. In those days, that was quite a large sum of money. We ended up with that amount after we had purchased the six tickets we needed to return to the Philippines, and we also covered other personal expenses. We knew what supplies we would need to buy in Manila and then ship them to our island, and we knew the price of airline tickets from Manila to our island.

We were certain that we had far more money than we would need.

The night before boarding our return flight, a married couple who were friends met us in our hotel. They did not have much money, but near the end of their visit, the husband pulled out a $20 bill and approached me to hand it to me. In an instant, several thoughts flashed through my mind, as he was about to give his offering. I immediately felt that it would be shameful on my part to receive that money from him when I had so much, and he had so little. I knew that it would be scandalous if he were to discover how much money we had at that moment.

Before I could tell him why I was not willing to receive his offering, another thought flashed through my mind, and I knew it was from the Lord. The Lord said, "To me there is no difference between $20 and $2,000. The only thing that is important is that you are faithful with both amounts. Receive it from him." When I considered what the Lord said, I realized that the main difference between $20 and $2,000 in the eyes of the Creator is the printing on those paper bills. I had no idea whatsoever of the enormous importance that our friend's $20 offering would play in our return to our home in the Philippines.

We arrived in Manila and purchased the things that we would need, without squandering any money. We then bought our airline tickets to fly to our island. Upon arriving there, we purchased six bus fares for the six-to eight-hour ride to the small town where we would hire a boat to take us and our cargo to the Bible school, another six-hour journey. The owner of the boat informed us of his price, and it was the normal amount. When we arrived on our beach and paid the owner for his services, we had a total of $0.75 left to our name. That $20 offering was just as important as the $2,000, because without it, we would not have arrived back home! I was reminded that faithfulness with the $20 is just as important as faithfulness with the $2,000.

CHAPTER 14

God Is Still Interested in Geography

God spoke to Abraham to offer his son, Isaac, in a specific place. That place was Mount Moriah because 2,000 years later, the heavenly Father would offer *His* Son in that exact place. From Deuteronomy 12 to the end of the book, God spoke to Israel over 20 times about the place that He would choose to place His name, the place where His temple would be built. He exhorts Israel to offer their sacrifices in that place and in no other. Again, it was the place where an infinite sacrifice would be offered about 1,400 years later—the sacrifice of His Son, Jesus Christ.

In the New Testament, we see in many ways that the God of the Old Testament has not changed. In fact, at the very end of the Old Testament, God Himself declares, "For I am the LORD, I change not . . ." (Malachi 3:6). His guidance in the life of the apostle Paul revealed that He is still interested in geography. He forbade Paul from preaching in Asia, and also in Bithynia, and then He led him to dedicate his efforts in Macedonia (Acts 16:6–9). Paul preached in Athens and there was almost no fruit. He then left Athens and went to Corinth, and the Lord instructed him to remain there because He had many people in that city (Acts 18:1–11).

In Guatemala, my wife and I learned by experience that the Lord is still interested in the geographical location of any work that He chooses to raise up. After spending six months doing nothing in Guatemala but seeking the Lord and studying Spanish, the Lord began to send us people who were hungry for God. We began to have meetings in our living room, but we soon outgrew that option.

We had come to know a Christian lady who made a living in real estate. Her name was Grace. I called her and asked if she knew of a place that we could rent for our growing congregation. She thought that she knew the perfect place. It had been a school, and had a number of buildings on the almost two-acre property. When we arrived there, we immediately knew that it would be perfect for what the Lord had said He wanted to do in Guatemala. We knew that a ministerial training center was part of His plan, and this property was ideal for both a church and such a center.

There was only one small problem. The budget of the church was a long way from being able to afford the rent that the owner was asking for the property, and she had made it clear that the price was not negotiable. As we drove away, saddened that we were in no position to rent the place, I mentioned to Barbara that it would have been perfect. She responded immediately, saying, "If that is the place that the Lord wants us to have, He is able to keep it for us until we have the finances to rent it."

Grace did help us to find a house that we could afford with a much larger living room than ours, so we began meeting there. After a year had passed, we outgrew that living room also, but the owner allowed us to knock down a wall and almost double the size of the meeting area. Another year passed, and I called Grace again, asking if she could think of another place for us. She hesitated for a couple minutes, and then it finally dawned on her, and she said, "The place that I took you to two years ago is still available. Would you like to see it?" That was very good news and now the church did have the necessary income to rent it.

We arrived at the property again, and began to look at the buildings. When I opened the door to the office building, something happened that has only occurred two or three times in my life. My eyes were opened, and I saw the Lord standing inside. He said to me, "I have been waiting for you!" At that moment, the Lord erased any doubt. I knew that He had chosen that place for us. This occurred on a Saturday, and we did not see any rush to close the deal before the following Monday morning.

However, the next morning, as I was sitting at my desk, getting ready for the Sunday morning service, the Lord spoke to me very clearly, "Call Grace and tell her not to show the property to anyone else, and that she should consider it rented as of this moment." I don't normally do business on a Sunday morning, especially when I am getting ready to preach, and it was 9:00 a.m., one hour before our service began. Also, I knew that Grace would be getting ready to attend her own church, and I did not want to bother her with such a call.

The Lord spoke exactly the same thing again, so I finally went to the phone and made the call. I said, "Grace, I am calling to let you know that as of this moment that property is rented. Please do not show it to anyone else." Grace was a very jolly lady, but I did not know just how jolly. I heard one of the loudest outbursts of laughter on the other end of the line that I had ever heard. She said, "Marvin, don't worry! I will not show it to a single soul. Do you realize that I have been working for two years trying to rent that place, and have not had a single offer? I am sure that no one will be interested in it before tomorrow!"

We hung up, but later that afternoon Grace called me back and was very moved. She said, "I cannot believe what happened after you called me. Within an hour, three men arrived at my door, with money in hand, and wanted to sign a lease for that property. Then, after our church service ended, one of the elders came up to me and said that they had decided to rent that place for a school. I told both parties that it was already rented. It was a good thing you called this morning!"

God's ways are past finding out! The poor owner of the property lost two years' rent, because God had decided that that place was for Hebron Ministries, and He made sure that no one else rented it before we were ready to do so. It was a very desirable property, as the two other parties that day confirmed.

We Do Not Need the Money!

By now, the will of God was so crystal clear that we wanted to talk to the owner to see if we could buy the place instead of renting it. We did not have the money, but we knew by experience what the Provider can do even when there is no provision. So, we asked Grace to arrange a meeting with the owner. I remember the scene as though it were yesterday. We were seated in the living room of her mansion, and I asked her, "Would you consider selling us the property instead of renting it?" She answered, "What are you offering?" I said, "We would like to buy it for $200,000."

The owner got visibly perturbed and offended, and she was clearly angry. She looked at me with a glare and almost shouted at me, "We do not *need* the money. Don't ever talk to me again about buying that property unless you are offering at least $500,000!" In that moment, the Lord said to me, "Ask her to lease it to you for 10 years, and I will take care of her." She agreed to a 10-year lease, and the deal was closed.

For the next three years, we spent much time and money improving the property in many ways. We even demolished some of the buildings and replaced them with new and much better facilities. We were well aware that if the owner ever showed up, the sale price would be increased, because our investments had greatly increased its value. But we knew that the Lord had said He would deal with her.

Near the end of those three years, I received a call from her. She explained that they had gotten into a business in the United States, and that it was requiring a large investment that they did not have. She wondered if we were still willing to buy the property. I assured her that we were willing. I did not have to twist her arm. The Lord had already done that, and we settled on a price of $144,000, just $56,000 less than the $200,000 that I had offered her three years before, an amount that had offended her. It was also $356,000 less than her lowest price of $500,000 three years before. She did not say it with her words, but she clearly declared with her actions, "We *need* the money!"

By the way, the Lord had twisted her arm so much that she not only agreed to a much lower price, but she also had a meeting with the Lord, and became a Christian. We later became very good friends with her and her husband, and when they saw what the church was doing, they were very thankful that they had sold the property to us. Also, the Provider provided the money we needed to pay cash for the property, and the money came from Guatemalans, not from the U.S.

We Need More Land

The work continued to grow spiritually and in number. Besides this, the Lord spoke to us about beginning an orphanage and also a grade school and high school. Sometimes, the Lord cannot permit a work to grow because pride would come in, and the Lord is more concerned about His messengers than He is about success. Near the beginning of the work, when the church had about 40 members, the Lord asked me, "Would you be proud if the work grew to 400 members?" I answered, "Lord, how could I be proud with only 400 members?" He then asked, "Would you be proud if the work grew to 4,000 members?" I answered, "Lord, how could I be proud about having 4,000 members in the church when there are millions who have never heard the gospel and who are lost?" I realized that one secret to walking before Him in humility is to see what we have *not* accomplished instead of seeing what we *have* accomplished!

Adjacent to the property that we had purchased, there was vacant land. It was part of the only farm that was remaining in the city of Guatemala, where there were more than 2 million inhabitants at that time. Today, the city has over 3 million inhabitants. According to our plans, we could do what the Lord was calling us to do if we could purchase from the owner about three-and-a half-acres. The owner of that land was a corporation with seven board members. However, those members were members of one family, and the matriarch was the leader. I got in touch with her, and asked if we could buy the land we needed. She said she would present it to the board, because they would have to vote on it. She contacted me a few days later to let me know that the vote was seven to zero against selling us the land.

Another year passed, and again I asked the matriarch if they would consider selling us the land once more. Again, the vote came back seven to zero against selling it. Upon outgrowing the meeting place that we first used on the original property, we enlarged and improved another building and moved the church into it. A year later, I again contacted the matriarch and again the vote was the same.

We then rented a commercial auditorium outside of our property when we outgrew the second building. After a time, the auditorium was full, so we went to two services on Sundays. Each year for seven years, I asked the matriarch to present the board with our request once again. Of course, we were praying that the Lord would choose for us, and touch the hearts of the board members. For six years the vote came back the same. On the seventh year, she contacted me and was quite excited. She said, "This is a miracle! This time the vote was seven to zero *in favor* of selling you the land, so we can draw up the contract."

Within days, we began work on six buildings on our new property. We were very pressed for time, because we needed to complete four large structures for the grade school and high school, and it was almost time for classes to begin. We had only three months to do so. During those months, we had 100 construction workers involved. We started the school on time in temporary facilities, and soon moved into the new buildings. We also continued the construction of a home for boys that would finally have three stories and 80 different small bedrooms, so that each boy would have his own room.

Finances began to come in like we had never experienced before. They came from many different sources, but they were all from members of the church, and not from the United States, with the exception of two very small offerings. At the end of a year of building on the new property, I added up all the bills that we had paid for material and labor, and the total was well over one million dollars. We were *very* surprised, and we remembered what the Lord had asked me when we were in Tokyo—"If you had a million dollars, would you buy that camera if it were not My will for you to buy it?" We saw just how easy it is for the Lord to provide a million dollars, and we rejoiced in Him! He can supply *all* your needs!

CHAPTER 15

God, Demons, and Haunted Houses

An infallible proof of the existence of God is the existence of demons and fallen angels. If they are real, then their Creator is real also, and the Bible is, once again, proven to be true. Personally, I have had some experiences with demons that I will share in this chapter.

The Window That Opened by Itself

As I already explained, between our second and third year in the Bible institute, my family and I moved to a property in a very remote area of upstate New York. We were there to help with the physical preparations for a new Bible institute to be opened. The man in charge had obtained a property that included a number of first-class brick buildings. The main building had four stories. No one had lived in the facilities for the previous 20 years. Before that, it had been a tuberculosis sanatorium.

My wife and I, along with another couple, were the first ones to actually live on the property. It would be three months before others would move in. We began living there in the month of May, and New York still has some cold weather at that time of the year, but there was no heating system. In fact, there was no electricity and no water either. It was a trying time, especially with two very small children.

Everything was rusted, nonfunctional, broken or unusable after so many years of neglect. The hinges on the windows were rusted shut, since they had never been opened for at least 20 years. My father came to visit us in the month of July. We were standing in front of the four-story brick building and chatting. It was a hot day, and there was not even a whisper of a breeze. No one was living in that building. Our friends and we were living in another building, and, as was usually the case, there were no visitors on the property except my father. Suddenly, on the far end of the fourth floor, one of the windows began to open slowly, with an enormous amount of creaking from the rusty hinges. We looked up and witnessed what was happening. Once the window was fully opened, we could see plainly that there were no hands moving the window, nor was anyone inside. After a minute or two, the window slowly closed with the same loud creaking.

My father was in a state of shock. He knew that it was a supernatural event. I was not at all surprised, because the property had many demonic manifestations that our friends and we had witnessed quite frequently.

We Will See About That Tonight

It is very important for believers to know that demons have absolutely no power to do anything against us without God's permission. If God gives the enemy permission, as He did in the case of Satan's attacks on Job, it is only to bring us into a new and greater blessing, and the enemy's evil designs will be limited by God's mercy and sovereignty.

On a Sunday night in the Philippines, I preached a message to the students regarding our total victory over the powers of darkness. It was a joyful time, as we saw the glory and privilege it is to have the Creator living within us, as a result of the new birth. No wonder the apostle John, speaking about the powers of darkness, declares, "Ye are of God, little children, and have overcome them: because greater is he that is in you, than he that is in the world" (1 John 4:4). On our way out of the meeting, I heard what was almost an audible voice challenging me. It said, "So you have the victory? We will see about that tonight." I responded immediately and said, "Yes, we will see about that tonight."

I went to bed and began to sleep very soundly, but right at midnight I was awakened by something, and I immediately saw that a black demon was standing beside the bed next to me. It was about six feet tall. The Holy Spirit instantly spoke through me. I knew it was the Spirit, because He quoted precisely a verse that I had never memorized, and barely knew existed. It was Psalm 59:14—"And at evening let them return; and let them make a noise like a dog, and go round about the city."

The enemy recognizes the voice of the Spirit and can never ignore a command from Him. Instantly, the demon turned toward the door in our bedroom that led to the outside. As he walked toward it, I saw a line of very small demons following him. At the precise moment when he went through the door (without opening it), our dog began to make a specific noise that dogs sometimes make when they are very troubled. It is a combination of a howl, a whine, and a whimper, and it includes a strange noise that is a little bit like the sound of singing. Many of us have heard such a sound from dogs at one time or another, and it is a very eerie sound. Of course, it might not have been our dog at all that was making the sound. It might have been the demon itself. Our dog had never made that sound before that moment, and it never made it again afterward, during the almost three years that we had her. Someone might say it was a coincidence, but my own eyes saw the demon, and there was no coincidence in the fact that as soon as he went out, a noise like a dog was heard very loudly.

The Spirit had commanded him to make a noise like a dog, and that is precisely and instantly what happened.

The Holy Spirit responded to the demonic challenge that I heard when I left the Sunday night meeting, and we definitely "saw about that" during that night, and the enemy was humiliated! Demons are real, and so is our God!

White Magic Turns into Black Magic

Some years ago, I was visiting a church in the U.S., and the pastor asked me to help him deal with a woman who was about 60 years old. She had attended the church for many years, but my pastor friend had recently begun to pastor that church. The woman was involved in what is called "white magic." It uses supernatural powers or magic for supposedly good purposes. In the case of this woman, a person had been murdered in that area, and the police believed that the body had been dumped in a lake. The lake was quite large, and the task of finding the body would have been enormous, but this woman, through her white magic, showed them where the body was.

However, she had asked the pastor to help her, because pots and pans were flying through her house at night, and she was afraid of getting hit by one of them. Her white magic had turned into black magic. We went to her house, and she showed us some incredible proof that she was definitely involved in something supernatural. One example, out of many, was that she showed us a common Kleenex that had what appeared to be a black and white photo impregnated into it. She explained how it got there. She said that during her spiritist séances demons appeared and used a dip pen and bottle of ink that she kept nearby during her contact with the demons, and they made photos on Kleenexes. On one of them, there was a photo of one of her dead relatives. Anyone could see that it was something supernatural, because any ink on a Kleenex will blot immediately. It would be impossible to even make a simple drawing on a tissue, much less a photo of a person who was already dead!

The woman said that she wanted to be delivered from the demonic manifestations that she had been accustomed to for years. We prayed with her, and then gathered up her things related to spiritism and took them out to a wooded area and buried them. However, she was like the owners of the demon-possessed girl in Acts 16:16–20. When Paul delivered the girl from demons, her owners got very angry because she no longer had the demons that enabled her to be a soothsayer. The lady whose things we buried decided that she wanted to continue practicing white magic, and she wanted her things back. As far as I know, she never got them back.

Haunted Houses Do Exist

In Leviticus 14:34–44 the Bible talks about leprosy being in a house. Some students of the Bible believe that leprosy is a symbol of sin, but a house is not sinful. Rather, a house can be the home of evil spirits or demons, just as a person can be also. In this passage, we see that some houses can be cleansed and some cannot. Obviously, God decides.

My wife and I, along with three of our children, spent a few days in a house that had been unoccupied for some time, like the buildings of the sanatorium I mentioned. There were clearly evil spirits that were staying in that house. They were not happy with Christians invading their territory. At first, they would awaken me by tickling my arms or face. Once I was able to ignore that irritation, they would start physically jerking my arms or legs during the night. In a few days, I was able to even sleep through that. But finally, one night, I was awakened when the entire bed was shaking. Once fully awakened, I assumed that my wife was making some very vigorous and forceful movements for the first time in our married life! When I looked over at her, she was sound asleep, and was not moving at all. Not only was I wide awake, but at that time the spirits appeared, and I saw them clearly. There were four of them.

Much has been written on the subject of "Lincoln's Ghost" in the White House, and many respectable, political people who have stayed in the Lincoln bedroom, have claimed to have seen his ghost. If only a couple of people had this experience, we could attribute it to imagination or hallucinations, but there are simply too many to ignore the reality of the spiritual problem that exists in the White House, at least in the Lincoln bedroom.

What Can We Conclude?

Over the years, my wife and I have seen many very clear manifestations of demons. We should all recognize that since demons exist, as the Bible reveals, it is therefore logical to believe that the Bible's accounts of demons are accurate. Since the kingdom of darkness clearly exists, then the Kingdom of Light also exists, as the Bible also reveals. In other words, our God exists as well. Demons do horrible things, but our God does wonderful and glorious things! There is no need to fear demons if we have a holy fear. As seen in the Bible, the fear of God brings us into every blessing that mankind desires. (See Proverbs 22:4 and Malachi 2:5.)

CHAPTER 16

God Used Water to Stop Pharaoh, and He Still Uses It

When God spoke to my wife and me about becoming missionaries in Guatemala, He said that He wanted us to have a part in raising up a company of worshippers. There are many types of worship in the Church world today, but God gives us this exhortation in Jeremiah 6:16: "Thus saith the LORD, Stand ye in the ways, and see, and *ask for the old paths,* where is the good way, and walk therein, and ye shall find rest for your souls. But they said, We will not walk therein."

Many Today Seek the New or "Modern" Paths

Many sectors of the Church today have chosen what they call "contemporary worship." Two synonyms for "contemporary" are "modern," and "present-day," therefore, it could rightfully be called "modern worship." Its leaders claim that it is a new, better, and greater revelation of worship than what the Church has had for the last 2,000 years. The problem is that heaven has never changed its worship or its way of worshipping, and King David received from God clear revelations of how heaven sings and worships. David discovered that God inhabits the praises of His people (Psalm 22:3). Would it not be an expression of pride to believe that we have better worship than what David had, or what the Church has had since it was founded by the Lord?

As a result of his experience in worshipping the Lord, David determined to have worshippers ministering continually, day and night, before the presence of the Lord (1 Chronicles 9:33, 16:4–6, 37). They employed the music of David and the musical instruments that God revealed to David (2 Chronicles 7:6). We are still commanded to sing the psalms—psalms, or music, that David received (Ephesians 5:19). We do not have the exact music that was used for the psalms in David's day, but we do have the same source he had—the Holy Spirit. We also should have spiritual fathers who can teach us the old paths.

The Tabernacle of David

Because of his heavenly worship, David was permitted to keep the ark of the covenant in a common tent, called the "Tabernacle of David" (compare 2 Samuel 6:17, Isaiah 16:5, Amos 9:11, and Acts 15:16). The ark was a wooden box covered with gold within and without. God commanded Moses to place in that box the two tables of stone on which He had written the ten commandments. The box was covered with a plate of gold, and the wings of two golden cherubim were stretched out over the plate.

The Bible tells us that the very presence of God dwelled between those cherubim (Psalm 80:1). His presence was on the ark in such a real way that it brought judgment on the Philistines after they had captured it. It was always covered, because no one was permitted to look on it or into it. When the Philistines returned it to Israel, many people decided it was their opportunity to look into it, and 50,070 died as a result (1 Samuel 6:19). In other words, and in a very real way, David had the very presence of the Creator in a tent on his property.

The presence of God that was upon the ark had dwelled in the Tabernacle of Moses for almost 500 years before David placed it in the tent. Moses' Tabernacle was an incredibly detailed and beautiful dwelling. Afterward, the ark dwelled in the Tabernacle of David for 30 years. Finally, it dwelled in the Temple of Solomon for another 500 years. Solomon's temple, to this day, was by far the costliest building that mankind has ever built. In today's dollars, just the gold used in it cost more than $200 billion.[10] A question that we should ask is, which dwelling did God prefer—the intricate one of Moses, the costly one of Solomon, or the simple tent of David?

The Dwelling That God Longs For

More than 200 years after David's tabernacle ceased to exist, God revealed the longing of His heart, and what He will do in the last days. He tells us, "In that day will I raise up the tabernacle of David that is fallen, and close up the breaches thereof; and I will raise up his ruins, and I will build it as in the days of old" (Amos 9:11).

David was a man after God's own heart, and he learned what it was that our God seeks. As Jesus tells us, the Father seeks people who worship Him in spirit and in truth (John 4:23). Far from being a desire that springs from divine pride, it is a desire that springs from infinite humility. God must humble Himself to look upon the heavens and the earth (Psalm 113:6), yet He is so humble that He wants to hear, from you, what you think about Him! Are you happy with Him? Only infinite humility could cause Almighty God to care about what *we* think about Him!

In light of all this, it is no surprise that in Acts 15:16, James explains what God was doing in the early Church. He was rebuilding the Tabernacle of David. God's people were once again

---

10 First Chronicles 22:14 tells us that David had prepared 100,000 talents of gold. A talent weighed 100 pounds, so there were 10 million pounds of gold. That is 160 million ounces of gold. At $1,300 an ounce, that comes out to be $208 billion. Added to this was all the gold that the princes and people gave later in 1 Chronicles 29:7, to say nothing of the million talents of silver that David gave in 1 Chronicles 22:14, along with the many very costly stones.

learning to build God's dwelling place, the place of worship. God was revealing to us that He is not drawn to the intricacies of the Tabernacle of Moses, although they reveal much truth, nor is He drawn to the riches of the Temple of Solomon. Rather, in His infinite humility, He loves the simplicity of the worship of anyone who is willing to tell Him that they love Him! Don't you want to tell Him how wonderful He is?

According to the prophet Isaiah, the Tabernacle of David is where the Lord will sit in His Kingdom: "And in mercy shall the throne be established: and he shall sit upon it in truth in the tabernacle of David, judging, and seeking judgment, and hasting righteousness" (Isaiah 16:5).

Now, in these last days, instead of rebuilding David's way of worship; instead of seeking for the old paths, the Church has the influence of the youth who have brought us modern worship. Are we to assume that they have received revelation from heaven regarding worship that David did not receive? Are we to assume that they are more spiritual than David and the great prophets who were in his kingdom, who also received music from heaven?

The answers to these questions are obvious. God has commanded us to seek the old paths and walk in them. We are not called by God to seek a "modern path." Will we be willing and obedient, or will we be like the rebellious ones in Jeremiah 6:16 who said, "We will not walk therein"?

Only Fathers Know the Old Paths

Over 40 years ago, my wife and I took the message of worship to Guatemala. We shared with the people there the worship that has been in the Church for centuries. We shared many details about how to rebuild the Tabernacle of David in our own lives.[11] Part of the reason we were aware of the

---

11 A course on this subject is available on DVD from Hebron Ministries. It is called "The Tabernacle of David and Praise."

worship of the old paths, is that, in our youth, we had some very old spiritual fathers, who themselves had some very old spiritual fathers in their youth. Their history went back to before 1900, and we witnessed how they worshipped the Lord. We learned the old paths from men who had walked in them for many years.

As a result, God began to raise up a company of worshippers, and we witnessed once again that God's presence fills His house when His people offer Him heavenly worship. After we had been in Guatemala for about four years, the pastor of the biggest church in Central America asked to see me. He said that they were looking for someone who could lead them into heavenly worship, and he had heard about our ministry. He asked me to be a co-pastor of his church, and to be in charge of the music, the musicians, the instruments that were to be used, and the worship in the church. He assured me that I would have complete authority in these areas. He proved to be a very honorable man, and for the next two years he was totally true to his word. He never once interfered in anything that I was doing regarding these areas. My time there ended after two years, because my wife and I moved back to the United States for a time.

All of the services of that church were transmitted on radio, and reached much of Central America. During that time, our teaching and guidance on worship reached many churches in many places. Part of the agreement with the pastor was that I would continue to pastor my own church also. There never was a problem with this arrangement. One Sunday morning, I was in my office getting ready for our service when I heard the singing and worship of a church near our property. I was amazed to hear them worshipping in the ways of the old paths that they had received from the radio transmissions. I was also very thankful to the Lord that He had opened that door, and that *He* was raising up a company of worshippers in many places!

Now Comes a Very Big Problem

A very big-name evangelist was coming to Guatemala for a short campaign. He was very much into contemporary music and contemporary worship. He would be holding his meetings in a very large stadium that holds thousands. I knew that his modern worship was going to negatively affect what the Lord had accomplished in Guatemala in the area of worship. The thousands of pastors and leaders who would be there would almost certainly reconsider what they had been hearing through the radio transmissions from the big church. How could they avoid thinking that this great evangelist had surely discovered the path to success, and that God must have been approving his music and methods? Many would surely ask themselves, "How could he be so successful if he is not walking in the old paths?"

When we began the Sunday morning service in our church, I explained to the people what was at stake, and the great damage that the afternoon meeting in the stadium could do to the Body of Christ in Guatemala. That meeting was the main event of his short campaign. I asked the church to pray that the Lord would somehow intervene so that the wrong message would not be given to Guatemala. As soon as I shared that, a spirit of intercession fell upon the congregation such as we had never experienced before. Everyone really cried out to the Lord with fervor. I was amazed and thankful for their reaction.

Now Comes a Very Divine Answer

After our service, an American brother who was working with us at the time, came to me. His parents were visiting him in Guatemala for the first time, after he had been there for years. His parents knew that I was a pilot, and that we had access to an airplane. He had told me that they were leaving the following Tuesday, and wondered if I could show them

Guatemala from the air on Monday? I told him that I would be happy to do so.

However, when he approached me after the service, he was very apologetic, and explained that he had made a mistake, and that his parents were leaving the next morning. He asked if I could give them the ride during that afternoon. I told him that it would be fine, because I definitely had no plans of being in the stadium for the campaign. So, we went to the airport for the flight. We took off and climbed above a layer of clouds.

When we got above the clouds, we could see a good portion of the nation. At 10,000 feet of altitude on a clear day, one can see for more than 100 miles in any direction. Above the clouds that day it was very clear, and we could see that there was a low-level layer of clouds that covered most of the nation. There were not even any breaks in the clouds, so my passengers could not see a single thing in Guatemala.

There Was, in Fact, One Thing That They Saw

I told them that it was unfortunate, but that the only reasonable thing was to return to the airport and land. They agreed. When we turned around and looked back toward the north and the airport area, we were very surprised to see that there was one, and only one, storm cloud in the part of the nation that we could see. It was a huge pillar of cloud that ascended to well over 40,000 feet. The low-level clouds were like a smooth white carpet, and poking up out of that carpet was an enormous, well-formed pillar that was only about 1,500 feet across. I had never seen anything like it as a pilot. It is almost a law regarding clouds and weather that if there is *one* storm cloud, there will be others as well. I have never seen any exception to this, even though I have seen *many* storms.

As we got closer to the airport, I realized that I would have to fly around the pillar of the storm to get on the final approach course for landing. As I tipped the wings to make the turn around that pillar, we all could see the first and only break in the cloud covering below us. To my amazement, my tipped wing was pointing down through that break in the clouds, directly at the national stadium where the evangelistic campaign was being held.

When we landed, and I arrived back to my house, I turned on the radio, and, at that moment, I heard the evangelist saying that he would preach under an umbrella in the light rain, and then have the concert after the preaching. He said that they had done that before in other places.

It was not until later that the entire scenario came out, both on the radio and also from the people who were there. As they were ready to start their evangelistic campaign, the musicians began to uncover their instruments. Just as they were almost ready to start playing on them, a flood of water came pouring down on them, and they were forced to quickly cover their instruments again. Within minutes, there were four inches of water standing on the stadium grounds. After they covered their instruments, the rain slowed to a drizzle, and the evangelist began to speak under an umbrella, explaining that he would preach first and have the music afterward. That was what I heard him saying when I arrived home and turned on the radio.

During his message the drizzle ended, so the musicians went back to their instruments after he had finished speaking. They got to their instruments just in time for another flood of water to come pouring down from that one and only storm cloud in the entire nation. That ended the campaign.

Several people who were there told me that when they drove away from the stadium they were amazed to discover that the streets were all completely dry within three city blocks of the stadium. I was not surprised at all. I had seen it from the air. Rather, I was amazed at how God had answered the intercession of the church that morning. He simply shut down the whole project, so that there was no negative influence placed into anyone's heart that day. God stopped Pharaoh with water, and He stopped that negative influence with water. God is amazing and wonderful! Oh, how we need to pray and intercede more! God responds to the cry of His people, and answers our prayers. He will answer your prayer at this very moment!

CHAPTER 17

God Will Do Great Things in France

Barbara and I, along with two of our children, visited France some years ago. We were using public transportation in Paris, and when we were approaching a bus stop, we saw that the bus we needed was about to depart from the stop. We began to run down the sidewalk toward the bus, but a small group of very unkind young people were walking toward us, and it was obvious that they were purposely moving over to run us off the sidewalk. It did not seem to be a big problem, so we simply moved off the sidewalk and onto the grass as we continued to run.

The Wrought Iron Picket Fence

I did not notice that there was a wrought iron picket fence close to the sidewalk, and my foot went under the pickets. Of course, the momentum of a grown man who is running is considerably more than what the foot can endure, and of course that momentum ripped my foot out from under the closely placed pickets. It felt like the fence had ripped my foot from my body. When I saw that I still had both feet, I knew that I had done some very serious damage to my foot, and I was quite certain that some bones had been broken.

Into the Emergency Room

At that point, we no longer needed to catch the bus. Rather, we needed to flag the first available taxi to take us to the nearest hospital that had an emergency room. When we arrived at the hospital, the taxi driver dropped us off in front of the hospital entrance. We had no idea where the emergency room was located, and I could not walk. At that moment, a man appeared on the scene, out of nowhere, and came up to us and asked us if we needed help. Later, upon reviewing what this man did, how he did it, and the extreme importance of what he did, we could see many reasons for believing that he might have been an angel sent by the Lord. We had no idea of the enormous problem facing us.

First, the emergency room was two blocks away. Second, as we will see in a moment, the hospital staff was on strike. Third, they were only accepting true emergencies, but they had to be emergencies that arrived in an ambulance in order to be accepted for treatment. This man must have known all this, so he called an ambulance, and instructed the driver to take us the two blocks to the emergency room, and the driver did so. That man obviously knew what was happening in the hospital, but even more amazing is that he knew how to call an ambulance, because all this happened long before the advent of cell phones! We did not even see him go to a phone from which to make a call.

Once the ambulance took me the two blocks to the emergency room, I was quickly cared for. I saw a doctor and two or three nurses. Of course, the doctor wanted an immediate X-ray of my foot. In my mind, I could see thousands of dollars floating out the window, but I knew that I had no choice, because my injuries had to be treated.

To the surprise of the doctor and nurses, the X-ray showed that there were no broken bones, but a visual exam confirmed that some very serious damage had been done to my tendons and muscles. On one side of my foot there was a swelling that was the size of half a baseball. The nurses treated the wounds, and bandaged my foot. The doctor warned me against walking on my foot for a couple weeks so that it would heal properly. He instructed me to obtain a pair of crutches from the pharmacy.

Of course, I did not need the doctor's warning about not walking on my wounded foot, because when I literally just *touched* the floor with *no* weight on my foot, the pain was unbearable. I had no doubt about my need for crutches, but I could not imagine what the rest of our trip would be like with me using crutches. One of my main concerns had to do with what it is like to travel with three women. Our daughters were older, and from the outset of the trip, they thought that they needed a lot of luggage. My wife had learned to travel light, but she still needed her luggage also. The problem was that there was a lot more luggage than what they could carry. Of course, initially that was not a problem, because in those days they still had a very strong father, but now the father was injured and would not be able to help with their luggage. In fact, they would have to help *him* for the rest of the trip with *his* luggage! These details would definitely slow us down.

We Are Very Sorry, but There Is No Way to Pay!

When the nurses had finished their work on my foot, and had wrapped it in a large bandage to cover the wounds, the head nurse approached me. I assumed that she was going to give me the bad news about the cost of my care in the emergency room. She approached me in a very apologetic way with her limited English, but as she continued to talk, I could not believe what I was hearing. She said, "We are very sorry, Mr. Byers, but today the hospital is involved in a strike. You see, almost no one is working, and we are only accepting emergencies. I am sorry to tell you that we do not have anyone here who can receive your payment for this attention. I hope you understand. It is only because we are on strike, so there will be no charge."

I could have told her that I understood perfectly their difficult situation, and that I did not want her to feel so badly, because I was feeling wonderful! Instead, I thanked her, and we quickly went to the pharmacy to buy a pair of crutches. We then hailed another taxi to go to our hotel. We checked in and went to our room.

The next morning, we all went to the hotel's breakfast, as I hobbled along on my new crutches. I lightly touched the floor with only the toes of my wounded foot, and the pain was as it had been the night before. At that point, I was very thankful for my crutches. We then went back to the room to have a time of devotions.

As we were praying and worshipping the Lord, the presence of the Lord came upon me in an incredible way. He began to speak to me about what He will do in France, and that He will visit the nation and touch many lives, bringing them into His Kingdom. Sincerely, I had had very little hope for the French. I knew quite a bit about their history, and some of it did not set very well with me, but at that moment, I saw that the mercy of the Lord is great enough to bring an enormous blessing to France, and the nation is going to experience a *mighty* visitation from God!

We were all standing at that moment, and I had my wounded foot doubled back and resting on the bed, so that I was standing on one foot only. During that personal visitation from the Lord, I felt that the Lord was saying to me that His immediate and complete healing of my foot would be a confirmation to me that I had truly heard from Him, and that He would do great things in France.

Upon hearing that, I cautiously touched the floor with only the toes of the wounded foot. There was no pain, so I put more of my foot on the floor. There was no pain, so I put all of my foot on the floor, and cautiously increased the amount of weight that I was putting on my foot. There was absolutely no pain, even with all my weight on that one foot. I took off the bandages, and the swelling was gone. I could put on my shoe again, something that had been impossible the night before. I walked out of the room, carrying my crutches, and I helped with the luggage. I left the crutches at the front desk of the hotel, and continued our trip for many more days without the slightest pain or discomfort.

God not only did a great miracle of healing, but He also put in my heart an assurance that France will be a very blessed country in the day of His great visitation. The instant miracle of healing was proof that He is the One who made the promise to bless France.

One other thing that this experience confirmed to us afresh is that all things work together for the good of those who love the Lord and who are called according to His purpose, as Romans 8:28 tells us. The enemy wanted to harm us by using those unkind young people who ran us off the sidewalk. It looked like our trip would be ruined, but instead, the Lord used the incredible healing of that terrible injury to confirm His message about France. That could not have happened without the help of those young people! Trust God to change your difficult circumstances into great blessings!

CHAPTER 18

The World's Biggest Shark?

"Brother Marvin, please come and help us. The monkeys are eating our garden!" This was the petition of the Bible school students in the Philippines on a Friday afternoon. I was the only one on the campus who had a rifle, so they asked me for help. They wanted me to go to the garden and shoot the monkeys. I knew that what they were asking me to do would be a futile endeavor, because I had learned long before that monkeys are very smart. When they are on the ground eating, they always have a guard in a nearby, tall tree. Amazingly, they also know the difference between a gun and a stick. With a stick, it is quite easy to get near them, but with a gun, they will be gone long before a person is close enough to shoot them.

Of course, I knew that the gun would scare them away, and that thereby I might save a few of the students' vegetables. What I expected is precisely what happened. The monkeys fled very quickly. The garden was next to a small river, and as I started back to my house, I noticed that fish were swimming near the surface of the river. I wondered to myself if it was possible to shoot fish. I took aim and shot. To my surprise, it was easy to shoot them. I shot only one or two, because they were too small to be of any value, and also because they were in the middle of the river, out of reach.

When I had almost arrived back to my house, I noticed a fish that was very near the shore, and it was large enough to provide my family with a meal. I took careful aim, and was surprised that my shot was perfect (a rare occurrence). The fish died instantly, but I had a problem. All I needed to do was to go to the shore of the river and pick up the fish. But between my position and the shore was a relatively steep bank that was about four feet long and muddy. I did not have on work clothes, so, I hesitated in getting mud on my good clothes. I spent about five minutes trying to devise a way to get the fish out of the water without slipping down the bank and sliding through the mud.

As I delayed, to my great sorrow, the fish began to sink and was pulled by the current toward the middle of the river, finally sinking out of sight. I returned home very sorry that I had not done whatever was needed to get that fish out of the water.

The next day, on Saturday morning, some of the Bible school students came to my door and said, "Brother Marvin, there is a good fish to shoot." I went outside with them, and there was a huge fish swimming back and forth in front of the Bible school. About 75 yards from the shore, there was an incredibly beautiful and untouched coral reef that ran parallel to the shore for a very long distance. The fish seemed to have been trapped between the reef and the shore. The reef extended up from the floor of the ocean, and its tops were about six feet below the surface (depending on the tide). However, between the reef and the shore, the water was 30 or 40 feet deep, more than sufficient for the large fish to swim in.

When I saw its dorsal fin protruding from the water, I was sure that it was a shark. I got my rifle and 20 bullets. Six young men had brought the school's large dugout canoe near to my house, and I got in. They began to paddle me out toward the fish. When we got to within about 50 yards from the fish,

I began to shoot toward it. Almost instantly, the fish began to swim toward us, and raised itself partially out of the water. Enough of the fish was showing that I could see that it was about five feet wide. I said to the boys, "That is not a shark. It is a whale, and I don't want to make it angry with this pea-shooter! Let's get out of here!"

They paddled us back to the shore, and we all got out of the canoe. At that point, two factors came into play. First, the fish kept swimming back and forth in front of the school. It seemed like it was challenging us. Second, I am an adventurist person, and I could not resist the challenge. I went back to my house and got 50 bullets. My semiautomatic rifle held 10 at a time, and I had two clips loaded with a total of 20 bullets. The boys began to paddle me toward the fish. This time, I began to shoot when we were still a long way from it. I could see when the bullets hit the water near it, so I began shooting a little in front of it, and then I slowly moved my aim upward so that I could see that the bullets were hitting the water behind it. Obviously, that way, some of the bullets were hitting the fish.

As we continued to do so, the fish began to swim slower and slower, and float higher and higher out of the water. We got nearer and nearer, and I was able to put the last shots directly into the fish. It was full of holes and was clearly dead. The ocean was red with its blood in a circle at least 100 feet in diameter. When we got right up to the fish, we were all shocked beyond words when we saw that it had gill slits. In fish, only sharks have gill slits. If you don't know what they are, you can search for "shark gill slits" in an encyclopedia.

At that point, the big question was how we would get the shark to shore. Very near to us was the school's boat, and I knew that the founder of the school had just recently placed 1,000 feet of nylon rope on the boat. I knew that all we had to do was tie that rope to the shark's tail, and then take the rope to the shore. By this time, there were more than 40 people watching this event. They would have been more than happy to help us drag the shark out of the water. My problem was a big fear of its tail because of what I had witnessed during the last few minutes before the shark was dead. As it swam back and forth, it would allow its tail to slowly come up out of the water, and then quickly lower it and cause it to slap the water. There would be an enormous splash with the accompanying sound that was enough to inspire fear in one's heart. The tail was probably a foot wide, and six to eight feet long. I realized that the fish could give one last death throe, as someone would be tying the rope onto its tail, and that it would be sufficient to break the person's neck.

Instead of choosing to tie its tail, I could see that its spine was very pronounced and extended about three inches above its body. I remembered that the school had a huge grappling hook tied to a rope that was used for construction. My immediate thought was that we would get that hook and throw it over the spine and hook the spine with it, and then drag the fish to shore. We quickly went to shore and everyone began looking for the hook. In the past it seemed that no matter what we were doing, the hook would always be under our feet, but on that day no one could find the hook.

After we had spent about five minutes searching for the hook, someone called to me and said that the fish had sunk. My heart sank with it. I gathered the six boys who had been rowing the canoe, and said, "Let's go look for it." The six boys grabbed some goggles, and rowed to the place where the fish had been. I don't know how I thought we could retrieve the shark, but I was desperate at that stage. They all got into the water and began swimming alongside the canoe, three on each side. I was standing up, and looking into the water, which was very clear. Suddenly, I saw the shark. Its tail was about ten feet down, and its body was on about a 45-degree angle downward. It was not swimming, and it was clearly dead. It was being moved along by the tide.

There it is!

I shouted to them, "There it is!" What happened next was something for the movies. All six boys turned into seals, as they flew out of the water and into the canoe, three from one side and three from the other. When they did so, they upset the canoe, and I went into the water. When I came up, I looked toward the sunken canoe, and saw six boys sitting in a row with their arms folded so that the shark would not be able to have lunch by eating anyone's arm. The canoe was submerged in the water, but since it was made of a very long hollowed out log, it did not sink, but the weight of the boys pushed it further down into the water. The sides of it were about three inches below the surface, so it looked like all six boys were sitting in the water in a perfect row. It was a very humorous sight, and I realized that they were not hunting for the shark, but rather trying to see it soon enough to get out of its way. I said, "Let's go back to shore," which we did.

I did not know what the world record was for the largest shark ever caught, but I had a very strong suspicion that this shark far surpassed any record. My wife took pictures of the adventure. One of her pictures was taken when we were right next to the shark, when I was putting the final shots into it. I was standing in the canoe, so it is easy to prove the length of the canoe, which was 18 feet, something we already knew.

I don't know why, but throughout the entire process of shooting that fish, it seemed to oscillate on its dorsal fin, first allowing the front part of its body to be out of the water, and then allowing the rear part of its body to be out of the water. Therefore, any given picture only showed about half of the shark. It might be hard to believe, but the pictures show that half of the shark was almost as long as the canoe that was next to it. Also, the part of the shark from its gill slits to the tip of its nose was never lifted out of the water. If you look at a picture of a shark, you can determine that about 25% of its length is from the gill slits to the tip of its nose.

If we decide to be *very* conservative in our estimates, then let's conclude that the half of the shark that was showing at any moment was four feet *shorter* than the canoe, in spite of what the picture shows. Therefore, we conclude that instead of being 18 feet long, the portion of the shark that was showing was only 14 feet long. This means that from its tail to the gill slits was 28 feet. Now, if we add the 25% of its length from the gill slits to its nose, the total length of the shark was about 35 feet. When I was actually next to it, I estimated that it was 36 feet long, and I was very accustomed to estimating lengths from 30 to 40 feet, because I did it almost daily when I was in the construction business and was measuring the lengths of rain gutters continually.

The shark was a hammerhead shark, and I later read in an article about sharks, that it is believed that hammerhead sharks reach a length of 36 feet, and unfortunately, I do not remember where I read that, but I *do* know from experience that it is true! Months later, someone who heard about my shark experience wrote to me and said that, at that time, the biggest shark ever caught had been 21 feet and 9 inches. My shark would have broken that record easily!

The Battle Had Just Begun

I returned home deeply frustrated. I did not know what the world record was for a shark, but I was quite sure that this shark would have broken it. I began to involuntarily review the whole event, beginning with the words of the students, "Brother Marvin, there is a good fish to shoot." I realized how completely foolish I was to not risk tying a rope onto the tail of the shark. Over and over, I reviewed every little detail of what had happened, and ended being convinced that I had been very foolish, as I derided my lack of wisdom.

I decided that I was not going to think about my loss any longer. However, the whole episode seemed to be on a video that kept rewinding itself and replaying the entire story over and over. I could not sleep that night, and the next day I earnestly tried to stop the video from replaying itself, but I just could not do so. I spent another sleepless night, and the next day I came to the conclusion that I was under a spiritual attack. I spent that day rebuking and resisting the enemy, but the video just kept replaying itself.

On the third day, I knew that I was experiencing a serious problem. I was not able to pray or meditate on anything of importance. On the third day, and for the first time, I finally looked up and asked the Lord what *He* was saying. For three days, He had been waiting for me to ask Him that question! He answered instantly in a way that I could never have imagined. He said, "Do you remember the little fish? Because you did not learn your lesson with the little fish, you lost the big fish. You were sorry that you had allowed the little fish to sink instead of pulling it out of the water immediately, at all costs, but you were not sorry enough to learn that a dead fish will float for only about five minutes. In life, if you do not learn the little lessons day by day, then you will fail when the big issues come up. Also, in life there are times when you must risk all to gain all."

Of course, this last part is something Jesus explained in a different way when He said, "For whosoever will save his life shall lose it; but whosoever shall lose his life for my sake and the gospel's, the same shall save it" (Mark 8:35). I was not willing to risk my life by tying a rope to the tail of the shark. Therefore, I lost an incredible opportunity. If the shark would have been a world record, then many people would have come to see it. As a result, we would have had the opportunity to share the gospel with many. How many times do we lose incredible spiritual opportunities because we are not willing to lay down our lives, our plans, and our rights to do the will of the Father?

I also learned another lesson from this experience. Speaking of the suffering of hell, in Mark 9:44, Jesus declared, "Where their worm dieth not, and the fire is not quenched." In the Bible, the fallen human nature is likened to a worm. For example, the Lord referred to Jacob, the supplanter and deceiver, as a worm (Isaiah 41:14). In hell, the fleshly, fallen human nature will never die. It will never be forgotten. In hell, a person's entire life will pass before them in detail, and they will see every time they rejected the gospel and the truth, and every mistake they ever made, and they will deride themselves and declare what fools they were.

In hell, people will determine to not think about their lives anymore, but the video of their entire lives will continually rewind and replay forever, revealing every detail about why they are in hell, and how easily they could have been in heaven for all eternity! The worm of their worldly, fleshly, sinful life will never die and will never be forgotten by them. Along with the torment of the fire, Jesus emphasizes that this also is one of the great torments of hell. During those three days, I experienced what this torment is like. Jonah was in the belly of a big fish for three days and three nights, but I had a big fish in my belly for three days and three nights!

Consider with me the incredible details that God had to ordain in order for me to have this experience:

1. Monkeys had to come to the school's garden, and it had to happen on a Friday afternoon, when the students were there to care for it and also there to protect it.

2. The students had to think of asking me to help them by shooting the monkeys.

3. On my way back from the garden, something I had never before considered had to occur to me—to attempt shooting fish.

4. When I got near to my house, God had to send a large fish near the shore. During three years of living beside that river, I never saw even one large fish anywhere, much less near the shore.

5. I had to aim perfectly to kill the fish instantly, or it would have swum off.

6. God had to place that fish near a steep bank along the river. That was the only steep bank on the entire river, and it extended for only a few yards.

7. The very next day, God had to send a huge shark in front of the Bible school, and inside the ocean's coral reef. Something that never happened before or after during our years there.

8. The students had to notice it and think of asking me to shoot it.

9. After shooting at the fish several times, the fish did not swim away.

10. After seeing how big the fish was, and getting back to the beach, I had to reconsider and decide to try again with more bullets.

11. God had to blind the eyes of dozens of people who were looking for the grappling hook. It was there, but no one could see it.

12. God had to allow me to be in torment for three days because of a fish, something that happened to Jonah, but I am *not* comparing myself to Jonah in any way! The entire experience was designed to teach me some important lessons.

Are you learning *your* lessons in life, and will you risk your life by giving it to the Lord? If you risk all in God, you will gain all (Revelation 21:7).

CHAPTER 19

Our Hairs Are Numbered

Jesus said, ". . . the very hairs of your head are all numbered" (Matthew 10:30). Why would God be interested in something so trivial as numbering our hairs? It is not an issue of being trivial. To understand why, let's assume that we were to ask any normal adolescent, who has faithfully received his education, how much is two plus two? We would not conclude that he is interested in trivialities if he immediately answers, "Four." Rather, it is impossible for the adolescent not to know how much two plus two is. God is infinite in every way. For example, He is infinite in power, in authority, and in knowledge. Therefore, it is simply impossible for Him *not* to know every detail about everything, including the numbering of our hairs.

Jesus made the statement regarding our hairs being numbered in the context of the Father's care over us. In fact, He says that not even a bird dies without the Father knowing. He then declares that we are of more value than many birds (Matthew 10:29–31). He cares for us even in the smallest details of life. He is not overloaded nor disinterested when we ask for help with the little things of life. In fact, in some ways, He is greatly glorified when He reveals Himself by helping us with a very small thing, because it reveals how infinite He is.

It reveals that He is able to get involved in the smallest matters that affect our lives, and not only be involved in our great issues. He can number our hairs, watch over us, and care for the birds, as easily as knowing what two plus two is.

The Lost Spring Is Found

Years ago, I was preparing to mow the grass in our lawn. It was long overdue, and the grass was very long, but when I started the garden tractor, and tried to mow, I realized that it was not working properly. I soon noticed that an important spring was missing. Somehow, it had fallen off somewhere on our property. In those days, we used the garden tractor for many jobs, and I realized that the spring could have been lost anywhere on our property of several acres. I looked for it for some time with no success. I was quite concerned, because in those days, to obtain a replacement spring was going to require a week or ten days. I knew that the grass would end up being longer than what our machine was designed to cut.

I continued to search one area after another. As we so often do as human beings, I turned to the Lord as a last resort, instead of as a first resort. I finally prayed, "Lord, You know exactly where that spring is. Would You please help me find it?" Without the least bit of exaggeration here, I can say that I had literally no sooner finished praying, when my eyes fell on the spring. It was off the path and in some grass. I was looking for it only on the paths, and I would never have looked for it somewhere off one of the paths and in the grass.

I not only gave the Lord much thanksgiving, but I stood in awe of His greatness and care. In some ways, I was amazed about this miracle even more than I had been amazed about even greater miracles in the past. Why? Because, in a new way, I saw the greatness of our God revealed in the smallness of man. I realized that He is able and willing to help us in the smallest of matters, and that doing so does not become a burden to His workload!

When It Is Time to Leave, Leave Immediately

I spent three years in the Philippines with my family, teaching in a Bible institute to train future Filipino ministers. One day, after we had been there for over two years, the Lord spoke to me this message: "When I tell you that it is time to leave the Philippines, then leave immediately, and do not allow anyone to convince you to stay longer."

I thought that that was a strange message, and I basically forgot about it. At the end of the third year of classes, we felt that our time in the Philippines had ended, and that it was time to permanently return to the U.S. I told the founder of the work about our plan to leave. He began to give me reasons for why I should stay longer. It was then that I recalled what the Lord had spoken to me almost a year before, so, without telling him what the Lord had spoken to me, I tried to kindly explain that we knew it was time for us to leave.

We had no idea of how important that message from the Lord would prove to be. Ten days after our departure, the worst typhoon in the history of our island hit where the school was. We had donated our house to another missionary couple, and they had already moved in. When the typhoon hit, the entire campus was inundated in three or four feet of water. That depth of water had entered our house, and the couple placed chairs on the dining room table and were sitting on them, as the water rose a little above the height of the table.

As I mentioned before, our house was near a small river that came down from the mountains. About 50 yards before it reached our house, it turned 90 degrees and emptied into the South China Sea. After the storm had ended, and the storm surge had flowed into the ocean, our friends took pictures of what the river had done. Because of the enormous amount of water flowing from the mountains, the river no longer turned 90 degrees. Instead, it had dug out a new channel that came right up to the corner of the house before it turned to the ocean, and the new channel was about 15 feet deep. It went straight down from the foundation and wall of the house. It was as though someone had used a bulldozer and cut away the earth, leaving a 15-foot wall right up to the house. It was a miracle that the river did not continue for another 30 feet before turning to the sea. The heavenly bulldozer could have easily carried the entire house into the sea, along with those who were inside, sitting on the table! When I saw the pictures, I realized that if we had disobeyed the Lord and remained there, we would have had no guarantee that we would not have been swallowed up by the river and sea.

Others lost their lives in that typhoon. In the jungle behind us, extremely primitive people lived. Most had never seen a white person, and some of them wore almost no clothes. When the typhoon struck, they all decided to climb the mountain to reach a higher and safer place. The highest point on the island where we lived is almost 7,000 feet above sea level, a seemingly safe place to be.

There were 243 in the group that decided to ascend the mountain, but one of them had been exposed to the Christians at the Bible school. He was convinced that God was with the school. He told the group that being with the Christians would be the safest place. No one else was convinced, so he *descended* while they *ascended*. Tragically, because of the enormous amount of rain that was falling, there was a landslide in the place where the group was climbing, and all 242 were buried alive. Although one man at the Bible school did die when a wall fell on him, it was not the man who descended to be with the Christians. Out of the 243, he was the only one who survived, and he did so by descending! He had decided to hide his life in the presence of the God who promised those who trust in Him that in the time of judgment ". . . there shall not an hair of your head perish" (Luke 21:18). He came to trust in the Lord who had numbered the hairs of his head.

What a spiritual lesson this story teaches us. Satan said, "I will ascend . . . I will be like the most High" (Isaiah 14:14). In his pride and self-assurance, he lost his spiritual life and his position in heaven because he tried to ascend. Afterward, in the Garden of Eden, he gave Eve the idea that God did not want her to be like Him. This was obviously the conclusion that he reached when he attempted to be like the most High and was cast down. If God did not want anyone else to be like Him, then why did He decide to make man in His own likeness and image? What Satan did not understand was that to be like God we must descend, not ascend.

Although our God is high and lofty, yet He dwells in the low place with the humble. He declares, "For thus saith the high and lofty One that inhabiteth eternity, whose name is Holy; I dwell in the high and holy place, *with him also that is of a contrite and humble spirit* . . ." (Isaiah 57:15). Jesus descended continually, as Philippians 2:5–11 describes. He loves the low place, and was the most humble Person that ever lived. The inheritance that He is offering to His people includes Canaan, a word that refers to a low place, a place of humility. That is where He will dwell with us forever!

Do you seek the high place of success, honor and position, or are you willing to humble your heart and allow God to choose for you?

CHAPTER 20

All Things Work for Our Good

For many years, our ministry was blessed with an airplane that I, personally, flew to places in most of North and South America. One trip that we often made was between Guatemala and Texas. Often, the trip involved both ministerial and practical purposes. We were able to combine speaking commitments with the purchase of equipment and supplies for the ministry in Guatemala. As more and more laws were passed by the U.S. Congress governing entry into the country, those trips became more and more complex.

An example is what happened to my wife and me in February 1995. We landed in McAllen, Texas, and as always, the U.S. Customs officers were the first to meet us (rather than to *greet* us). As usually occurred, their first question was, "Are you bringing in more than $10,000?" Bringing in more than that amount is permitted, but it requires that a report be filed regarding the details. The value of any foreign currencies at the current dollar exchange rate must be included as part of the $10,000. Since we were bringing in money to buy things for the ministry in Guatemala, we actually had $8,500 with us. Therefore, I answered no. The head Customs officer then asked my wife the same question, and she answered no. He then asked me the same question again, and got the same answer. He then instructed us to go into his office to fill out the paperwork for Customs.

On our way into the office, Barbara remembered that we had left quite a few Mexican pesos in the airplane. The reason was that just after they had been donated to the ministry in December 1994, there was a historic devaluation of the peso. The peso lost half of its value overnight. At that time, we heard that the U.S. was going to help prop up the peso, and that it would recover some of its value. Therefore, we decided to leave the pesos in the airplane with the hope that they would recover some of what they had lost. On this particular flight, we had forgotten that they were onboard.

We both realized that if we included the pesos, then we actually did have more than $10,000 with us. When we got inside the office, I told the Customs officer that we had some pesos with us that we had forgotten about, and that we did actually have more than $10,000 with us. At that point, he began to act like a Keystone Cop.[12] His first reaction was to tell me to take one step sideways to my right. I did so. Then, he explained what I faced. He said, "You have just lied to a U.S. Federal Customs officer. The result is that I can confiscate your airplane and everything in it. Also, you face a prison sentence of 5 years, and a fine of $5,000.[13] Tell me how much the total amount is. We will then count it, and if you are correct within 5% I *might* let you go."

During our 40 years of ministry in Guatemala, my wife has carried the burden of maintaining a very precise account of all the money that comes in and what it is used for. Therefore, I turned around to ask her how many pesos we had, because she knew and I did not. The officer shouted at me, "You can't confer! You can't confer!" This was actually the first crime that was

---

12 In the early 1900s there was a film comedy that featured completely incompetent policemen. Its name was *Keystone Cops*.

13 I do not recall the exact amount he said the fine would be. It may have been more than this.

committed that day regarding our case. By law, a family must report *together* the money that they have between them. He would not allow me to obey that law. I then asked him if he could tell me what the peso to dollar exchange rate was on that day. Being on the border, he obviously knew, but he refused to tell me, so I took a guess at how many pesos we had, and I took a guess at what the exchange rate was. He then told us to bring all our luggage and money inside, and that they would count it.

On the way out to the airplane, the other two Customs officers whispered to us that the agent who was arresting us was only looking for a promotion. They told us that he had busted an elderly couple that morning over just a few dollars. Many days later, when I talked to the head of the Customs department over that part of Texas, she told me that they had been having problems with that officer with regard to unjust arrests.

During the previous 20 years, prior to this experience, when my wife and I traveled, we would always keep our money in a portable diversion safe. There are still a number of options for diversion safes, but the one we used was a Gillette shaving cream can that looked exactly like the can that men used for shaving. The only difference was that the bottom of the can could be screwed off. Inside, the can was empty, so it could hold quite a bit of cash. When we got our luggage into the Customs office, the agent told us to give him all the money we were carrying.

Since the Customs officer wanted to see our dollars, as well as the pesos, we first opened the suitcase that had the portable safe, and handed him the Gillette shaving cream can that contained the dollars. Once again, the great wisdom and ability of the Keystone Cop were revealed. He took the can, and asked, "What is this?" Neither of the other two officers who continued to accompany him had ever seen such a thing. I had to show them how the bottom of the can could be removed. They were amazed! Imagine, the men who were trained to guard our borders against illegal smuggling had never seen such a thing. They were very possibly allowing illegal drugs to enter the country through diversion safes!

When they finished counting the money, it turned out that we had a total of a little more than $15,000. The amount I guessed was within 6% of being correct, but he said he *might* allow me a 5% error. He then confiscated all our money, and explained that we would not be able to recover it. He said that for humanitarian reasons he was going to return to us a little of our money. He ended up giving us one bill. Instead of giving us a bill in dollars, he gave us a bill in pesos that had a total value of $12. At the time, it might have been enough to buy our lunch. He then proceeded to inform me of the next step, explaining that he was required to hand my case over to the chief of the airport police. He told me that the chief of police would decide if they would handcuff me and take me to prison or not, and that we would have to wait until he arrived.

My wife and I sat together on a small, two-seated wooden bench while we waited for the chief to arrive. We felt like two sheep going to the slaughter. We talked about how utterly corrupt the whole process was, and that the man behind it was filled with ambition and condemned us for telling the truth. Then, Barbara said something that would be prophetic and extremely accurate. She said, "But all things work together for our good" (Romans 8:28).

The chief arrived and took me into his office. He saw the initial report, and asked, "Mr. Byers, what did you do?" I told him the whole story. He then looked at me intently and said, "Mr. Byers, you have done nothing wrong." About then, the Keystone Cop cracked open the chief's door and asked what he had decided. The chief said, "Mr. Byers has done nothing for which he should be arrested."

The agent then said to him, "But tell Mr. Byers that during the next seven years the Federal government could arrest him at any time." The chief's back was toward the officer, so he just rolled his eyes in contempt and said, "That is right, Mr. Byers, but I can assure you that you will not be arrested." That was the end of the proceedings, except that we had just lost over $15,000, at least we thought it was so. We appealed to the head of the Customs for that area so we could ask her to review and consider our case. We got an appointment for some time later. It was in a different city.

The First Indication of Divine Intervention

Fortunately, we had credit cards, so we were able to continue our journey, a journey that included staying in 10 different hotels along the way. As we were packing up to leave the last hotel, I picked up the portable safe to place it in our luggage. We always placed it on the bathroom countertop in our hotel rooms so that it would appear to be part of our toiletries. To my surprise, the bottom fell off when I picked it up. Upon examining it, I could see that someone had used a tool to pry open the can. They had broken the bottom off. I am sure that they were very content with the reward for their efforts—there was nothing but air inside! The Customs officer had, unknowingly, arranged that scenario. Of course, we never again used a diversion safe for our money. We realized that the thieves had discovered that tactic.

The Final Indication of Divine Intervention

We finally went to our appointment with the chief Customs official for the southern part of Texas. She was very kind and admitted that they were having problems with the officer who had treated us like criminals. She then explained that they were going to return all of our money, except for 10%, because the law required that 10% of all confiscated money could never be returned. We left her office rejoicing.

We had never rejoiced so much about losing money. Even though $1,500 was a considerable amount, we realized that the Lord allowed us to lose $1,500 instead of $15,000. If that corrupt Customs official had not confiscated the $15,000, most of the money we were carrying would have still been in the portable safe when the hotel employee pried it open. We planned on buying the things we needed just before flying back to Guatemala, so all of that money would have still been in that can.

I can definitely say that the Customs officer was corrupt. Why? Because eight years later, under the Freedom of Information Act, I was able to get a copy of the report regarding my arrest that he had sent to the Federal Customs office in Washington, D.C. In that report, he told eight bald-faced lies about the episode. One is that I had continued to lie until they did a search and found the true amount of money that I had, and another lie he wrote is that I resisted arrest.

God Can Use Any Vessel to Bless and Protect Us

Was all of this just a coincidence? Never once have we had problems with the U.S. Customs during multiple entries into the country during over 50 years. Never once in 20 years did anyone break open our portable safe. Only God knew that it would happen on that precise trip, and He allowed a corrupt officer to confiscate our money, so that we would not lose it all. We can definitely say that all things work together for our good, even when wicked people are involved.

Paul tells us, "But in a great house there are not only vessels of gold and of silver, but also of wood and of earth; and some to honour, and some to dishonor" (2 Timothy 2:20). God is always in control, and He can even use vessels of dishonor for His purposes. We all have vessels in our homes that we avoid touching. Among other things, they are used to remove trash and garbage. In God's great house, the Church and this earth, he has vessels that gather and remove trash and garbage. A man once told me that Satan is the Lord's garbage collector. At the time, I thought that to say such a thing was a bit strong, but I have come to see that the Devil does exactly that. People who do not choose the Lord will be gathered and deceived by him. So, when a corrupt Customs officer does his best to harm us, we can be sure that God is still in control and has something good in store for us if we trust in Him! Will you be gathered by Satan or by God? It is your decision.

Chapter 21

He Is the God Who Controls Storms

Jesus amazed His disciples when their boat was about to sink in a powerful storm, and with one command He immediately calmed the storm. The God who did so is still alive, and He still has total control over both natural and spiritual storms. My wife and I are witnesses of God's power to control even the worst of storms.

A tornado of historic proportions did enormous damage in East Texas, where we live, on April 29, 2017. It was rated as an EF4 tornado.[14] It was one of the largest tornadoes in recorded history. The average tornado is 200–300 yards wide, and remains on the ground for one to six miles with wind speeds of less than 110 miles per hour.[15] The center of the EF4 tornado in East Texas

---

14 See "April 29, 2017 East Texas Tornado Event," National Weather Service, accessed June 17, 2019, https://www.weather.gov/fwd/tornadoes-29apr2017 and "Tornado Facts and Information," accessed June 17. 2019, https://www.tornadofacts.net/tornado-scale/f4-tornado.html.

15 See "Tornadoes," Weather Explained, accessed June 17, 2019, http://www.weatherexplained.com/Vol-1/Tornadoes.html and "Tornadoes: The winds from these natural disasters wreak havoc on whatever they touch," National Geographic, accessed June 17, 2019, https://www.nationalgeographic.com/environment/natural-disasters/tornadoes/.

passed directly through our property.[16] As an EF4 tornado, its wind speeds were up to 260 miles per hour. It picked up cars and turned them into missiles, throwing them hundreds of yards away.

For a distance of one mile to the right of our property most houses were either destroyed or damaged. Also, for a distance of one mile to the left of our property most houses were either destroyed or damaged. Therefore, the tornado was at least two miles wide. The widest tornado ever recorded was 2.6 miles wide and it remained on the ground for 16 miles.[17] Our tornado was on the ground for 51 miles doing incredible damage along its entire path.

We live in a rural area, and there are not many houses that could be called mansions. But about a mile from our house there was a very large mansion that had been recently built. It cost more than $1 million to build. When the tornado approached, there were 90 people who were gathering there for a wedding reception. Most of them were able to fit into the owner's underground tornado shelter. When they came out, the only thing that was left of that brick mansion was a part of the rear wall. The entire house and all that was inside had been totally carried away. Only its cement slab remained. According to a fireman who was among the first to arrive on the scene, there were a number of dead people there, according to what he personally told our neighbor.

What God did on our property is a testimony to His greatness and also to His mercy. For the people in our neighborhood, it is also a testimony of God's kindness to Hebron Ministries. On the entire property there are sixteen structures, including four houses. The tornado uprooted an estimated 500 of our trees. Most of them were oak trees, and some of them had trunks that

---

16 When I refer to "our property" I am referring to both the property that my wife and I own, as well as the property that our ministry, Hebron Ministries, owns. It includes 87 contiguous acres, and more than half is wooded.

17 See Matt Daniel, "El Reno Tornado on May 31 Now Widest Ever Recorded in U.S.," *EarthSky*, June 5, 2013, http://earthsky.org/earth/el-reno-tornado-on-may-31-now-widest-ever-recorded-in-u-s.

were about three feet in diameter. They were enormous trees that were well over 120 years old. The tornado uprooted them as though they were twigs.

In the case of three houses that are in very different locations on the 87-acre property, the tornado came up to each house in all its fury, uprooting enormous oak trees right up to near the house. It then jumped over each house and continued to uproot enormous oak trees on the other side. It did absolutely no damage to any of the three houses.

In the case of the fourth house, the tornado approached it with its powerful winds as shown by the damage it did just before reaching the house—leaving a small building that housed a well in little pieces. Then, just before jumping over the house, it tore off about one fourth of its shingles. The truth is that instead of being a loss to the ministry, it was a gift. Why? Because in a few days, we had planned to put a new roof on that house, but because of the many missing shingles, the insurance company paid to replace the entire roof.

What about the other eleven structures? Except for that well house and one other very small storage shed, the other structures were not even damaged. The storage shed measured 10 feet by 10 feet and we were really not using it, and it was crushed. The Lord knew that we needed a much larger shed, and the result was that the insurance company helped to replace it with a new 24 feet by 30 feet metal shed that has become an enormous blessing. So instead of loss, there was blessing.

I will mention one other point. Most of the buildings are quite new, but one is an old barn that has a corrugated metal roof. Even before the tornado, a couple of the metal roof panels were missing. Each panel is 8 feet long and 4 feet wide. We were awestruck regarding the power and danger of an EF4 tornado. It removed one more of the metal panels, lifted it up over trees that are almost a hundred feet tall, and turned it into a missile that flew for hundreds of yards before landing. Imagine getting hit with something like that, to say nothing of being hit by a flying automobile!

A man who had been our insurance agent before retiring, was at home with his wife when the tornado hit their house. The next thing they knew, they were both outside in a field, slightly hurt but alive. Their house had totally disappeared. They surely can testify of the literal way in which Job 27:21 can be fulfilled—"The east wind carrieth him away, and he departeth: and as a storm hurleth him out of his place."

Some days later, a person located them, and gave them a document that had the ex-agent's name and address on it. They found it in the street near their home, thirty miles away from where the agent's house had been! What power, and also what thoughtfulness on the part of the many good people who still populate the earth!

That was just one of many stories of thoughtful and helpful people who did all they could to relieve the suffering of others. In our case, there were trees down all over the property. In fact, an oak tree whose trunk was almost three feet in diameter had fallen across our driveway, totally blocking it. Before I had time to do anything about it, a pickup truck stopped in front of our house, and two people got out and asked if we would like their help in removing the tree. After several hours of work, they had totally removed it as a favor. The terrible effects of that tornado actually did something very positive. It revealed that God still has people who love Him and who love others. Books could be written on what people did, as they sacrificed their time, strength, and money to help others.

Such natural disasters also show how God decides who is protected and who is not protected. As we enter the last days, how very important it is to live in a way that pleases our God, and to seek for His life and virtues to be formed in us. In no way am I saying that none of those around us whose houses were destroyed were not pleasing God. The Bible tells us that Job was a perfect man, and yet he lost everything in one day. God is the one who decides who survives difficult times and who does not, but we can and must hope in His mercy. Nahum 1:3 tells us that "The LORD is slow to anger, and great in power, and will not at all acquit the wicked: the LORD hath his way in the whirlwind and in the storm . . ." He decides! "Fire, and hail; snow, and vapour; stormy wind fulfilling his word:" (Psalm 148:8). He controls the storms!

Zephaniah 2:2–3 (NKJV) gives us divine counsel in order to prepare for the time that is near at hand: "Before the decree is issued, or the day passes like chaff, before the Lord's fierce anger comes upon you, before the day of the Lord's anger comes upon you! Seek the Lord, all you meek of the earth, who have upheld His justice. Seek righteousness, seek humility. It *may be that you will be hidden* in the day of the Lord's anger."

This passage makes it clear that even those who seek the Lord have no guarantee of surviving a time of judgment. However, the Bible *does* tell us that if we seek the Lord and end up not surviving the terrible day, then we will be with the Lord forever. Those who do *not* seek the Lord cannot expect that end!

Videos of the Historic Tornado

On our property, we have a number of closed-circuit video cameras that record all activity during a period of one month. When the enormous tornado passed through, our cameras recorded video footage from a number of different angles and locations. One of the most awesome recorded scenes was when the tornado passed over our house without doing any damage, and then, two pecan trees in our front yard faced its fury. They are about 25 feet tall. A few yards from the pecans was the oak tree whose trunk was almost three feet in diameter; it also faced the same fury.

It was impressive to see the pecans laid over on one side until their branches were touching the ground. At the same time, it seemed that the oak tree would remain standing, but suddenly it came crashing down. When the winds of the tornado finally passed by, the two pecans sprang to their upright positions, and were totally unharmed. What was the difference between the pecans and the mighty oak?

An interesting fact about pecan trees is that if their height is 25 feet, then their taproots go down 25 feet into the soil. They have a very deep root system. Regardless of their height, their roots go just as deep. Of the 15 pecan trees on our property, we did not lose even one.

Most of the more or less 500 trees that we lost during the tornado were oak trees. I learned two very amazing facts about oak trees, at least about the type we have on our property. I inspected and photographed the root system of many of the fallen oaks. Not even one of them had a taproot. Also, if the trunk was three feet in diameter, then the entire depth of the root system was only three feet; if their trunk was only one foot in diameter, then their roots went down into the soil only one foot. Their root system could simply not sustain the more than 200-mph winds that came against them. Imagine an oak that is 100 feet tall with roots that only go down three feet!

The spiritual lessons are very clear. The Bible compares trees to people. God's people are called "trees of righteousness" (Isaiah 61:3). The wicked are also compared to trees (Psalm 37:35). We know from history and from the Bible that mankind has faced, and will yet face, enormous spiritual storms. Whether or not we survive those storms without falling depends on what kind of a tree we are. It also depends on whether or not our spiritual roots are found in God, and if we have allowed our roots to go deep by seeking the Lord. May we also be like a pecan tree where no matter how high we rise, how much success we might attain, or how much people tend to exalt us, we will have humility that goes just as deep as our height.

If we follow the counsel of Zephaniah 2:3, there is hope regardless of the strength of the storms we might face: "Seek righteousness, seek humility. It may be that you will be hidden in the day of the Lord's anger." May we allow our roots to go deep in God, and our humility to be just as deep as whatever height we might reach!

CHAPTER 22

God Confirms His Word
with Signs Following

Speaking about the disciples, Mark 16:20 tells us, "And they went forth, and preached every where, the Lord working with them, and confirming the word with signs following." God still confirms His word with amazing signs. It might be a word preached to others or else a word He speaks directly to us.

God Confirmed His Word with an Earthquake

During our annual seminar in Guatemala City, Guatemala, on November 7, 2012, I shared a few important messages that God was speaking to His people. During the first session of the second day, I referred to the Guatemalan earthquake in 1976 that killed 23,000 people and left over one million homeless. It had an intensity of 7.5 on the Richter scale. After I finished sharing that session, we began a 30-minute break. Ten minutes into the break, another powerful earthquake hit Guatemala. It had an intensity of 7.4 on the Richter scale, basically the same intensity as the earthquake of 1976. It was a great and fearful confirmation to what the Lord was speaking to us!

He Confirmed His Word
That Was Embarrassing at First

In 1963 I was a student at the University of Michigan. I lived in one of the many, very nice dorms that the university had built for men and women. In those days, the women's dorms were about three miles from the men's dorms. Each one housed about 200 students. I lived on the fourth floor of my dorm, and that year, I had been chosen to be the athletic director for our house.

There were no elevators in the dorms. I imagine that those who were responsible for designing the buildings planned for at least some of the students to maintain good physical fitness. One day, as I climbed the steps toward the fourth floor, on the landing between one of the floors, I found a dime. I picked it up and continued to my room. In those days, a dime was worth almost what a dollar is worth today. As I entered my room, I felt that the Lord spoke to me to put a sign in the place that I had found it, saying that whoever lost it could retrieve it from me in my room. I obeyed what I believed was a word from the Lord. I put my name and room number on the sign.

I realized that the Bible tells us that we are supposed to attempt to find the owner of anything of value that we find. Of course, since I was the athletic director for the entire house, everyone knew who I was. It was one of the most embarrassing and humiliating things I had ever done in my entire life. I also realized that almost anyone who would have seen my sign would have laughed me to scorn, believing that I was unbelievably absurd! Of course, no one ever came to me to claim the dime, and I definitely did not expect anyone to do so.

For 35 years, on a few occasions I recalled that event, and I always wondered if I had truly heard a word from the Lord, or if it was only a fruit of my own narrow-mindedness. In 1998, after I had preached in our Sunday morning service, a young man came up to me, asking for counsel regarding a decision that he had to make. His decision regarded obedience in a small thing, and sincere honesty in the issue. It was going to involve a humiliation.

I shared with him about my experience with the dime, and how embarrassed and humiliated I was to obey what I felt the Lord wanted me to do. As I finished telling him the story, I took a small step backward, and felt something under my shoe. I moved my foot and looked down. It was a dime. I picked it up and gave it to the young man, and knew deep in my heart that, at that moment, after so many years, the Lord was confirming His word that He had spoken to me at the university. He was also showing me that, through the dime, He had been testing me regarding obedience, honesty, and a willingness to be humiliated. I rejoiced greatly in my heart, and I still do every time I remember the sign that I had placed on the wall in that dorm. He had definitely confirmed His word with a clear sign that followed 35 years later!

The Lord Gave Us the Name "Hebron"

When my family and I moved to Guatemala as missionaries in 1978, there were new groups of believers springing up all over the nation. God was visiting the nation. He had brought repentance through the earthquake of 1976. Very often, the only way for God to bring repentance to a nation or even a person, is for Him to first bring great crushing.

However, these new groups were being called by the names of their leaders. When a believer would ask another believer where they went to church, they would often answer, "I go to the group of So-and-So." My wife and I did not want the church that the Lord was founding through our ministry to be called by our name, so we began to pray about the name that the Lord wanted to give us. Throughout the Bible, names are clearly *very* important to the Lord. If a name comes from the Lord, then it is prophetic, and He will fulfill its significance in us if we continue to seek Him.

What we had been considering were names that involved God's mercy, but we just did not have any clarity about God's will. After some time, we dropped the subject, and we did not talk about it for weeks. Then, one night, as my wife and I were having our evening devotions, suddenly, and for no apparent reason, I heard the word "Hebron" in my heart over and over. I did not say it with my mouth, because I began to suspect that it just might be the name that the Lord wanted to give us. I did not want Barbara to be influenced by hearing me speak the word Hebron. When our devotional time ended, and we were in bed, and Barbara was almost asleep, I asked her, "Have you felt anything about a name for the church?" She responded immediately, saying, "What do you think about the name Hebron?" I asked her why she said that, and she told me that she had no idea why she had said it, and that she was almost asleep at that moment. She told me that she had not even been thinking about Hebron in the Bible, but it just popped out of her mouth.

We knew then that the Lord had given us *His* name for the ministry. By giving the ministry this name, He was showing what He planned to do with this ministry. Hebron in the Bible is where Abraham lived in the Promised Land for many years. It was the place where King David experienced his second and third anointings. He was anointed as king in Hebron over only the tribe of Judah, and later, he was anointed in Hebron again over all Israel. From those events in the Bible, we see that Hebron is associated with the place of the anointing. In the Bible, the anointing refers to God's presence. We knew that the Lord was calling us to prepare Him a dwelling place so that His presence would be among us.

What Hebron Means

The Hebrew word for "Hebron" means "association." The definition of association is "a relationship, an alliance, a union, a link, a bond, a tie." Psalm 133:1–2 gives us an idea of why David was anointed in such a place. That Psalm tells us, "Behold, how good and how pleasant it is for brethren to dwell together in unity! It is like the precious ointment upon the head, that ran down upon the beard, even Aaron's beard: that went down to the skirts of his garments." Where there is unity between the brethren, the anointing oil of God's presence comes upon us.

In Isaiah 10:24–27 God comforts His people, saying that the Assyrian would come against them, but that his yoke on them would be destroyed because of the anointing of God's presence. This was actually fulfilled, at least partially, in the days of King Hezekiah, when 185,000 Assyrian soldiers woke up in the morning as dead men.

While living in Hebron, when Abraham heard that his nephew, Lot, had been taken captive by the four most powerful kings on the earth at that time, he arose from Hebron with men that were "confederate with him" and defeated those kings with 318 trained servants (Genesis 14:13–16). The anointing of God's presence was upon those united men, and God's presence will always bring down the most powerful attacks that the enemy launches against our souls.

To this day, the literal city of Hebron is still a very important place in Israel. The tombs of Abraham, Isaac, Jacob and their wives are still there, and many tourists visit them each year. So, when God chose to give us the name of Hebron, we were very thankful and greatly surprised.

Just a few years later, God confirmed His word to us when He gave our ministry the name "Hebron." He did so by confirming our spiritual link to the literal Hebron in Israel in an amazing way. On March 3, 1983, we decided to begin a Bible school in Hebron to train spiritual leaders. The next day, I read in the newspaper that the day before (on March 3), Israel had decided to begin a religious training center in Hebron to train their spiritual leaders. That was an *enormous* decision for Israel, because Hebron was, and still is, an area of great conflict where the Palestinians lay claim to the entire city, and most nations of the world support their claim. There was an international uproar that lasted for weeks because of Israel's decision regarding a school in Hebron. The world said that Israel had no right to be involved in Hebron, much less to found a school there. Since we started the school in Hebron in Guatemala, there have been great battles also, but the Lord has fought every one of them. The enemy has said that we have no right to have a spiritual school in his territory, but in 2018, we had our thirty-third graduating class!

Blessings That God has Poured Out upon Hebron

Over the years, Hebron has grown in several important areas. After beginning the local church, we then began a Bible school where classes were given at night, and local people attended. Then, we began a Bible school where we had students from many different nations living on campus to receive a two-year course of studies. We later began a boys' home, and raised a generation of boys who are now men between the ages of 30 and 44. Some of them are on our full-time staff and are very great blessings. Two of them are, pastoring churches in South America.

We also began a traditional grade school and high school, and after 13 years, we changed to a homeschooling system in Spanish that is now in more than 20 countries. Because the teachers are recorded on video, and start with the very basics, children can study at home without any help, beginning in kindergarten and on through the twelfth grade.[18] The academic level of the school has been confirmed to be higher than almost any other schooling option. This has been confirmed in many places by means of the grades that our graduates receive on national tests in different countries. In addition, Hebron has founded many churches in different countries, and over the years, many pastors of already established churches have decided to be part of Hebron Ministries also.

18 In Guatemala, it is not called the twelfth grade, but it corresponds to the twelfth grade in the U.S.

Two More Confirmations that
God Gave Us the Name Hebron

When we first decided to put a website on the Internet, of course, we wanted our address to be www.hebronministries.com. However, years before we had even decided to launch a website, we had already noticed that someone else owned that domain, so we fully expected that we would have to use a different name. Over the course of several years, I checked the Internet from time to time, and always found that the same people continued to own that address that utilized the name Hebron. When we finally finished designing and testing our website, and were ready to launch it, we were trying to decide on an address for our website. We had several other names in mind, but just before we launched, I decided to look up the address we wanted to use one more time, just to be sure that it was still unavailable. To our great surprise and joy, the name was no longer in use, after it had been used for several years! So, our Internet address is www. hebronministries.com.

Later, in Texas, we wanted to register our name with the state so that we could do business in the state as a recognized legal entity. In fact, it is illegal to buy or sell property in Texas without being an organization or person registered with the state. I did not know that at the time. Of course, we wanted to do business in Texas under the name of Hebron Ministries. I called the state corporations office, and talked to an agent. She informed me that someone else already had that name in Texas. She gave me the name of the registered agent of the organization and his phone number and address. I called him and asked him if they were still using the name of Hebron Ministries. He said that they were not using it any longer. I asked him if he would give it to us. He said that he would ask the board and let me know their decision. I waited for several years for his call or letter, and he never responded.

After allowing years to pass without registering Hebron in Texas, one day the Lord spoke to me very plainly that I had been irresponsible in not registering Hebron. We had not broken any law, as yet. The Lord spoke to me in the late afternoon on a Friday. So, I determined to register Hebron on the following Monday morning. On Monday, I called the state office again, and asked the agent that answered my call what the closest options would be for using the name of Hebron Ministries. She answered, "Wait a minute, please." A few seconds later she said that the name Hebron Ministries was now available, because, as of three weeks prior, the state had sent a letter to the owners of that name, requiring information from them. Since they did not answer, they cancelled their use of that name. After years of waiting, just "by chance" I called the state at the very time when the name became available.

I asked the agent if there was some way to expedite our registry of the name. She said that I could do it that very day, if I paid a $20 fee for that service. I immediately paid the fee with a credit card, and the name of Hebron Ministries was legally registered in Texas that Monday.

We had a very important appointment for the very next day. It was to sign documents for the purchase of a property in Texas that Hebron Ministries was buying. I had absolutely no idea about the importance of what the Lord had just done for us by exhorting me to register Hebron Ministries immediately. I would have assumed that it was totally unrelated to this purchase. When we arrived at the title company, and sat down with the seller, as a legal formality the real estate agent announced at the very beginning that Hebron Ministries was a legitimate organization in the State of Texas. She said, "I verified it this morning with the corporation offices of the state, so Hebron Ministries has the legal right to buy this property."

After all was said and done, I asked the agent if it would have been illegal for Hebron Ministries to buy the property without being registered. To my utter amazement, joy, and thankfulness, she said, "It is a crime to do so, and would involve jail time." I did not tell her that Hebron Ministries had been duly registered for a total of one day! I could only thank the Lord for saving me from accidentally committing a serious crime. After I had waited for so many years, His exhortation caused me to register the name with

Texas just one day before I would have committed that crime!

This experience not only revealed God's mercy regarding how He can open the ears of someone who is deaf, but it once again confirmed in awesome ways, that He was the one who gave us the name. For those who are unbelievers, it should also reveal the reality of God's existence, and that He still speaks to men, if we are willing to listen.

CHAPTER 23

The Day of Small Things

The prophet Zechariah asks, "For who hath despised the day of small things? for they shall rejoice . . ." (Zechariah 4:10). I want to share a number of experiences that could be called "small things," but they demonstrated the sovereignty of God and caused us to rejoice. For most readers, they will be seen as more infallible proofs of the intervention of the Lord in our daily lives.

God Knows Where We Are

Sometimes we face difficult situations, and we are not sure if we are in the right place doing the right thing. I have experienced this a number of times in my life, and in those times, I have asked the Lord to give me *His* answer regarding my doubt.

One of those times was when I had to have an operation on my colon, not because of cancer or some other malady, but because of medical malpractice.[19] After the operation, I was in my

---

19 Malpractice occurs far too often. That is why doctors need malpractice insurance. However, I did not file a lawsuit. We should not try to get rich because of other people's mistakes. Of course, there are times when a lawsuit is in order, especially when the mistake would cost a person dearly, and sometimes for many years.

hospital bed, not being completely sure whether or not my need for an operation had to do with me not fulfilling God's perfect will in some way. At that point, I needed to make a cell phone call to one of our leaders. As I was talking to him, I suddenly heard the voice of my sister-in-law. She has a very distinctive voice, and I immediately recognized it. She was not talking to me, but rather, she was talking to one of her daughters. Any possible doubt about whether or not it was she who was speaking was quickly erased because she mentioned her husband's name during her conversation, along with the names of two of her daughters.

Some might respond that I was hallucinating from the anesthesia, or that I only imagined that such a thing happened. However, I received the anesthesia the day before, and I was out of bed, standing at the window of my room, and my wife was sitting next to me when it happened. I immediately told her the details of what I was hearing on the phone. *She* was not hallucinating!

The mystery of this event was beyond any natural explanation. First of all, my brother and sister-in-law are missionaries in Africa, and at the time that I was hearing her voice on my cell phone, they were in Africa. The call had been made at least one or two years before, when they were in the United States. I knew this for sure, because during the call that I was hearing she explained to her daughter that at that moment she and her husband were staying with one of their daughters who lives in the United States. In other words, it was a call that had been made long before.

I know a man who is a recognized expert in the installation and maintenance of national cell phone services. I asked him if it was possible in the natural for a one- or two-year-old cell phone call to be recorded, and then be heard again by someone. He assured me that it is totally impossible. I confirmed his answer with another cell phone service expert who told me the same thing.

At that time, I realized that God was doing a miracle to show me that He was with me and guiding me, and that He knew exactly where I was and what I was doing at that moment. After I talked with those experts, I was even more sure of my conclusions. Why would a stray cell phone call make me so certain? First, because it was a miracle that such a thing happened. Second, apart from family members, almost no one else in the world besides me would have recognized who was talking on that stray cell phone call that had been made a year or so before.

In order for me to recognize that a miracle was happening at that moment, four things had to occur. First, it was necessary that the call had to have been made by someone whose voice I would recognize. Otherwise, I would have assumed that the stray call was being made at that moment by someone else, and I just happened to be listening in. Second, the caller needed to be someone who was not even in the United States at the time, so that I knew that it was not a call that was being made at that moment. Third, according to the two experts with whom I talked, this has probably never happened to another person in the world. Lastly, that stray cell phone call came to *my* phone instead of going to someone else's phone. God's miracle confirmed to me that all was well!

God Knows the Future

During the first years of our Bible institute, a small group of our leaders prayed with each student who was about to graduate. Those who were involved in praying were free to express anything that they believed the Lord was speaking regarding the past, present or future in the life of each student. There are innumerable examples of God revealing the future work and/or ministry that He would accomplish through the different students. So many of those examples were fulfilled with such precision that there can be no doubt that the Lord was definitely showing the future.

One of those examples was spoken to a young man, and it seemed to be very unusual. The message was that the Lord would use that student to teach children about Noah's Ark. Some time later, he went to Africa to work as a missionary under the supervision of an older missionary who was part of our ministry, Hebron Ministries. The older missionary had become friends with a missionary couple who was working with a different ministry in the same city. After the young man had spent a good amount of time working with the older missionary, he earned a very favorable testimony.

At that time, the other missionary couple were planning to leave the mission field for a time, and they asked the older missionary if he could send them someone to teach a weekly class that they gave to a group of children. The missionary agreed to send the young man to teach the children. When he reported to the couple for their instructions, they explained to him that they followed a written curriculum in booklet form that involved different parts of the Bible. They told him that they wanted to continue with the curriculum, and that the next section that would be taught while they were away was Noah's Ark. Only God could have known that the children he would teach were on the other side of the world, and that someone would ask him to teach children specifically on that subject. So, in no way was this a self-fulfilling prophecy. Without a doubt, the young man knew that he was in the right place, at the right time, and that the Lord was with him!

God Can Use Events in Our Lives to Speak to Us

Very often things that occur to us, or that are said to us, will confirm what the Lord is speaking to our hearts. I could write a book on just such occurrences in our own lives, but I will share just two examples.

The first example occurred some years ago. For some reason, one morning during my devotional time, I began to think about a woman who had killed several of her husbands by putting strychnine into their food. This happened many years before, and she was finally caught. But what was interesting to me was how the human mind can recall a word so rarely used or even heard, such as "strychnine." I realized that I personally had probably never used that word even once in my entire life, yet it was in my vocabulary. Also, I was quite sure that I had never heard anyone else use that word ever since the story of the evil wife many years before.

No sooner had I thought along those lines than the phone rang. It was a fellow minister who was calling. I appreciated his ministry, and I had invited him to teach in our Bible institute. He had done so not long before calling me. During the course of our approximately three-minute conversation, he mentioned "strychnine." I was awestruck. I do not recall why he mentioned it, but at that moment, I knew that I had most surely received a message from heaven. Almost immediately, I understood why strychnine and this brother had been linked that day, and why I had been thinking about the wife who put strychnine into the food of her several husbands.

His wife was doing to him in the spiritual realm what that other woman had done to her husbands in the natural realm. She was killing him, ministerially, through spiritual strychnine, or in other words, spiritual poison. My wife and I knew that this brother's wife had some very serious spiritual problems, but we did not know what they were until I received his phone call. He did not understand why doors did not open to him, but she was the reason. She injected so much spiritual poison into any relationship that people reacted by shying away from him, even though he had something worth hearing. She had another spirit at work in her life that was destroying his ministry.

Sadly, there are many wives whose husbands have God's call to the ministry, but in many cases, God cannot use the husbands because of the negative influence of the wives. Of course, many times it is the husband who hinders the spiritual well-being of the family. However, a wife who has a godly husband needs to understand that she, too, must nurture her own spiritual life for him to accomplish God's purposes.

The second example I want to share regarding how God can use events in our lives to speak to us was very amazing. The name Studebaker came to me one day for absolutely no apparent reason. That name had not even crossed my mind for about 50 years. Only older people will recall what that name is linked to. Until March 16, 1966, it was a very respected and high-quality manufacturer of the Studebaker automobile. As a young man, I was never the least bit interested in their cars, and my lack of interest was obviously shared by most Americans—hence they went out of business.

The first amazing detail involved in my experience was the specific day when the name Studebaker came to my mind after not hearing the word for many years. The last Studebaker car rolled off the assembly line on March 16, 1966. When the name Studebaker came into my mind, it was almost the precise day of the 50th anniversary of that last car. One thing is certain, I had absolutely no idea when Studebaker stopped making cars. I do not even recall hearing the news that they had stopped making cars. Besides, there were very few of them on the road in those days. As the saying goes, "Out of sight, out of mind." This saying could be applied to their cars in those days. I can say with all sincerity that I had even forgotten that Studebaker used to be one of the manufacturers of cars and pickup trucks. Because of that, I was amazed that that name even came to my mind! Later, I was even more amazed when I learned that it came to me on almost the exact day of the 50th anniversary of the assembly of their last car.

The morning after thinking about those vehicles, I decided to take my wife out to eat for breakfast. On our way to the restaurant, we came upon a Studebaker pickup that was going down the highway. I could not believe my eyes. I doubt that I have seen any Studebaker vehicle on the road for at least 40 years, and I had just thought about their name the day before, after forgetting that it had even existed. Although it was amazing to see a Studebaker on the road right after remembering their name, it was doubly amazing because any Studebaker that is in good condition is worth thousands of dollars as a classic. Most owners do not want to expose so much money to loss by risking the destruction of their classic vehicle in a traffic accident.

What was God's message? First, only God could have reminded me the day before of a name that I had absolutely no interest in, and had totally forgotten, knowing that I would come upon one of those vehicles the next morning! He knows the future! If nothing else, this sequence of events is at least some indication of the reality of God. Second, only He knew that we would be traveling on that specific road *at the very moment* when that vehicle would be there. In our area, we have many options for eating breakfast, and they involve at least four different highways to reach them. For sure, this was a message that we were in the right place, at the right time, doing the right thing. One important message that I received is that I need to take my wife out more often. This is true for every husband, even if it is only to go out together for a cup of coffee. Married couples need times of fellowship.

And so ends the chapter on the "day of small things."

CHAPTER 24

A Powerful Earthquake Confirms God's Word for Ecuador

Torrential Rains

For many years, Hebron Ministries has had churches in Ecuador, South America. My wife and I have made many trips to Ecuador, and almost without exception, during each trip, enormous problems have arisen that have created considerable difficulties for us.

During one of our first trips to Ecuador, just before we were scheduled to fly back to the United States, a wide-body airplane crashed on the Quito airport runway. The debris required the airport to be closed for some days, including the day of our departure. Our airline rescheduled us to depart from Guayaquil, the second largest city in Ecuador. Our ministerial trip was centered in Ambato, Ecuador, which is a tourist center, located in the center of the nation. Normally, it requires about eight hours to drive from Ambato to Guayaquil. Since our flight was leaving early in the morning, we planned to arrive in Guayaquil early enough to spend a night in a hotel.

We departed from Ambato with plenty of time to reach our goal. We traveled on the highways that are normally used for that trip, but about an hour into our journey, as we traveled on a narrow road, we came upon traffic that was totally stopped. After some time, we learned that the road a few miles ahead of our position had been washed away by the torrential rains that had been falling for days. Our first thought was to turn around, but there were large trucks and buses behind us that were occupying more than half of the narrow road. Basically, all the drivers in front of us realized that it would be very difficult to successfully navigate the narrow spaces between the large vehicles and the edge of the road, especially since the road had no shoulder and was very muddy.

Along with everyone else, we just sat there, hoping against hope that they would somehow get the road opened where it was washed out, at least enough for the traffic to progress. That never happened, and after an hour or two of sitting in that seemingly impossible situation, I began to imagine what the world news would announce the next day. It would say that thousands of people were stranded on a narrow road in Ecuador, without food or water, and that helicopters were flying in the essentials, because there was no way out!

After a couple of hours, everyone in our car decided that we should turn around, and try our best to return to the beginning of that narrow road. We all understood the risk of trying to squeeze by the large vehicles on a slippery, muddy road with no shoulder, and with deep gorges in some places. We knew we faced a few miles of stranded traffic behind us. To make a long story short, after five hours on the road, we were finally back in Ambato, where we started our journey. There was another, longer way to reach Guayaquil, but we were now running out of time. We would have to drive all night, and we knew we could not afford to miss a single turn on the longer route.

In that area of Ecuador, there was a very special brother of African descent who used to drive taxis along the route we were going to take. We called him and asked him if he would be willing to go with us so that we would not miss any turns. He agreed to do so, and I did the driving. We knew that we had to drive quite fast in order to arrive at the airport in time for our flight. Our speed, along with the many dangers on our route, was a little hair-raising. We sometimes say that a person turned white from fear or nervousness. Later, this brother described our trip graphically. He said it was the first time in his life that he was actually a white man! This brother was on the edge of his seat for many hours, but we made the flight!

The Indigenous People Close the Highway

On another trip to Ecuador, on the very day that we were scheduled to fly back to the United States, the indigenous people blocked the highway between Ambato and Quito. They were demanding things that they thought only the government could give them. Once again, it looked like we might not make our flight. The only way to do so was to leave very early in the morning before the road was blocked. We ended up arriving in time for our flight, but having had very little sleep.

This Time the Truckers Blocked the Highway

Then there was the time that we were in Ecuador when the truckers decided to block the road between Ambato and Quito. They were not happy with something that only the government could change. Once again, the only way to arrive in time for our flight was to leave very early in the morning before the road was blocked. And once again, we ended up arriving in time for our flight, but having had very little sleep.

Then There Was the Bicycle Race

During another trip, and once again on the day of our departure, the main highway was going to be closed because of a bicycle race. As the above experiences show, frequently the highway to Quito was closed on the very day of our departure. Therefore, each time, we got very little sleep the night before, because we had to begin the two-and-a-half-hour drive to the airport very early in the morning.

And Suddenly, a Powerful Earthquake

On one trip to Ecuador a fellow minister and I traveled together, and my wife stayed behind in Dallas. My friend had spent years in Ecuador, pastoring a church there, and he was well aware of the incredible problematic events that occurred in Ecuador during basically every trip that my wife and I had made to that country. On a Saturday morning, he and I were eating breakfast on the tenth floor of a large hotel in Quito. We began to discuss how, almost without exception, huge events occurred during our trips. We both agreed that it seemed to be an indication that the Lord wants to do something very special in Ecuador. Whenever and wherever the Lord is planning to move, the enemy tries to block and hinder His plans. When we face problems, we should not always assume that it is because we are doing something that God is not blessing. It could well mean that we are simply involved in a spiritual battle.

As we ate breakfast that morning, we both expressed our doubt about what the huge event would be on this particular trip. We had literally no sooner expressed our doubt when a huge earthquake hit Quito. It was a 7.0 earthquake on the Richter scale. It occurred on February 9, 2013.[20] The building began to sway back and forth an incredible distance. At the time, to me it felt like it was moving at least five or ten feet in either direction.[21]

20 See "7.0 Earthquake Rocks Colombia," *USA Today*, February 9, 2013, https://www.usatoday.com/story/news/world/2013/02/09/earthquake.../1904581/. This earthquake was centered in Colombia but covered much of Colombia and Ecuador.

21 See https://gizmodo.com/video-the-tallest-apartment-building-in-america-sways-1651431... The tallest apartment buildings in the U.S. sway four to five feet from the wind. Obviously, they would sway much more from a powerful earthquake.

The people who were eating in the restaurant immediately jumped up and began to run toward the stairs. My friend and I were the only ones who did not move. That was because we both had lived in Guatemala, and had experienced strong earthquakes. We learned a few details that apparently the people who were in the restaurant that morning had not learned. First, an earthquake almost never lasts for more than 45 seconds, and that would not be enough time to run down 10 flights of stairs. Second, if the building collapses, there is more chance of surviving if a person is on a higher floor. That way, the rest of the floors do not come crashing down on them. Third, when the earthquake causes buildings to sway from side to side, the buildings are less likely to collapse. Such earthquakes are called horizontal earthquakes. A vertical earthquake jolts the building up and down and is more dangerous because all the higher stories act like a giant hammer on the lower stories. Of course, *any* number 7 earthquake is very powerful, and can do terrible damage.

There was one other reason that I did not move when the earthquake hit, and I believe that my minister friend felt the same. We had just talked about the incredible things that happened on almost every one of our many trips to Ecuador, and that they were a strong indication that God was going to do wonderful things in that country. About one or two minutes before the earthquake hit, we had been asking ourselves what great event would occur on the trip we were on. When the earthquake hit, we knew that the Lord was speaking very clearly, confirming what we had just expressed moments before. We knew that He was in control of the earthquake, and by sending the earthquake at that moment, He was speaking of blessing and not judgment. He was confirming that He will do great things in Ecuador. We rejoice for the blessings that will come upon the inhabitants of that beautiful country!

We should also remember that many spiritual seeds were planted in that country. One example was the deaths of five missionaries who attempted to visit the Auca Indians there.

They flew into their territory in a plane piloted by Nate Saint, and they were all martyred by the Aucas on January 8, 1956. Jesus, speaking of His own life that He would soon lay down, said, "Except a corn of wheat fall into the ground and die, it abideth alone: but if it die, it bringeth forth much fruit."

The Lord did not forget those five grains of wheat that were planted among the Auca Indians. Later, the wives of the five martyrs went and lived among the very Aucas who had killed their husbands, and they led many of them to the Lord. Their conversions marked the end of the revenge killings that occurred frequently among the tribesmen. A wonderful outcome of this story is that some of the very tribesmen who killed the five men became close friends to the families of the five. One of the main leaders of the Aucas became a minister to the tribe.

Our small sacrifices that we faced during almost every trip we made to Ecuador do not compare with the sacrifices of those five men, their wives, and others who have given their lives in Ecuador. However, what we have faced definitely gives a message—God will do very great things in that nation.

CHAPTER 25

He Is Also a God of Judgment

God is *very* longsuffering. The Bible tells us that He, ". . . is longsuffering to us-ward, not willing that any should perish, but that all should come to repentance" (2 Peter 3:9). However, it is common for men to misunderstand what God is doing when He delays judgment on sin. As King Solomon wrote, "Because sentence against an evil work is not executed speedily, therefore the heart of the sons of men is fully set in them to do evil" (Ecclesiastes 8:11). This is what is occurring throughout the world today as mankind sinks ever deeper into a moral cesspool where every imaginable vile sin is promoted and even praised by the promoters of evil. God delays judgment to give us a chance to repent, not so that we will continue in sin.

Most assuredly, the Final Judgment will come, and this is what atheists ignore, and sometimes mock. However, what we sincerely believe to be true, does not change the truth, whether we are right or wrong. We cannot say to a judge who will rule on a traffic fine we may have received, "But, your honor, I honestly believed that the speed limit was 70 miles per hour. I did not see the sign that said it was only 30 miles per hour!" No normal judge would say, "Since that is what you believed, we will cancel the fine."

In the Final Judgment, the Judge of the Universe will not say to an atheist, "Since you sincerely believed that there was no God, and that you would not have to give an answer for your sins, I will allow you to enter heaven!" It is our responsibility to know the traffic laws if we are going to drive, and it is our responsibility to know the laws of God in this life. That is one reason He gave us an instruction book that is called the Bible.

One awesome reality in life is that God allows judgments to fall upon sinners even in this present life, without waiting until the Final Judgment. Sometimes it is a divine attempt to bring a person to repentance, but sometimes it is a divine decision to put an end to a sinful and twisted life. King David wrote, ". . . God is angry *with the wicked* every day" (Psalm 7:11). If a wicked person is allowed to live even one more day, it is because of God's great mercy. Also, ". . . when thy judgments are in the earth, the inhabitants of the world will learn righteousness" (Isaiah 26:9). In His kindness, God uses judgments to bring us to Himself.

The following experiences we have had reveal how God can put a period to a wicked life and also how He calls people to repentance.

God Said,
"The Bullets of My Judgment Are Flying"

When I was in business, the main thing my company did was to install aluminum rain gutters on houses. It was a very lucrative business in those days for those who were willing to work hard. My primary source of customers came through contractors who built houses, or remodeled them.

One day, one of the contractors for whom I did work called me. He said, "I have a customer who is very unhappy with the installation of his gutters. You did not do the job, but please go and do whatever repair needs to be done." I arrived on the scene of the "crime," and asked the owner of the house to show me the problem. It was a two-story house, and he took me to one side of the house and pointed up to the gutter on the second floor. I could not see anything out of order.

He explained that the gutters had been installed a year before, and that he did not realize that there was a problem until the following spring. He explained that he had used a ladder to wash his new gutters, and he noticed a scratch on one of them. It couldn't be seen from the ground, but he wanted it to be changed immediately. I told him that I would let the contractor know so that he could decide what to do. So, I called the contractor and told him the "horror" story. He decided to do nothing.

A few days later, he called me and pleaded with me, saying, "That man will not leave me in peace. He calls every day and insists that his gutter must be changed. Please go and change the gutter regardless of the cost."

I drove to the man's house, and got out of my truck, and was headed to his front door to give him a piece of my mind. It was then that the Lord spoke to me very clearly. He said, "This very day, the bullets of My judgment are flying, and if you rise up, you will catch one of them. Just change the gutter in meekness, and do not even knock on his door." I believed the Lord and I obeyed Him.

The next day, the contractor called me and said, "You will not believe this. You went to that man's house in the morning, and at three in the afternoon he died!" I was not surprised, but I was very thankful that the Lord gave me the meekness to change that gutter without rising up against the owner. Did I believe that God took that man's life because of his unreasonable demand about his gutters? Not at all. I realized that this was simply the way he had lived for many years, and that this unreasonable demand was a last straw for the Lord, and He decided to put an end to his life. God's spiritual bullets of judgment took him away.

A Baby Drowned in His Milk

One of the guidelines that I established for members of the church that I pastored for many years was that no one could ask another member for financial help, or even a loan. Also, no one who had money could give financial help or a loan to another member. Was this cruel? Was I unconcerned about the needy? Not at all. I explained to everyone that if there was a needy person in the congregation that they should tell me or another leader about their need. I would then decide what should be done.

For example, if the "needy" person happens to have two late-model cars, I would probably tell him to sell one so his need would be met. But if he is truly needy, then the church will help him by meeting his need in the best way. There is a reason for this guideline. If in a church, the poor can approach any person who has money and ask for help, then the man with money will soon feel very uncomfortable in that church. Also, if a man with money could become a banker in the church, then he will end up with tremendous influence over the lives to whom he has given or loaned money. It is not wise to permit either situation in a local church.

Of course, if a rich man wants to help a poor member, then he is free to do so, but he needs to do it through the leadership so that the poor member does not feel indebted to him. He can give his money to the pastor, and then the pastor can give it to the needy person, as an anonymous offering. Also, anyone can put an offering into an envelope and write on it that it is an offering for the person he names. We always make sure that every penny of every such offering goes to the person for whom it was given.

This way of operating was established in the early Church in the book of Acts. The offerings were laid at the feet of the apostles, and they made distribution to the needy. "Neither was there any among them that lacked: for as many as were possessors of lands or houses sold them, and brought the prices of the things that were sold, and laid them down at the apostles' feet: and distribution was made unto every man according as he had need" (Acts 4:34–35).

Although this was a clearly established guideline in our church, a young mother began to tell other ladies who had more resources than she did, that her baby had no milk, because they had no money to buy it. Of course, some of the ladies gave her money. After all, who would be willing for a newborn to starve to death? My wife and I talked to the young mother, explaining to her that she had ignored the guidelines, and that she must not tell anyone else such a thing. We knew that what she had told the ladies was not true.

A week or so later, she did the same thing, and we talked to her again, forbidding her to ask for money from other members. Not only did we know that her baby had milk, but we also knew that she was using the money that had been given to her to buy for herself some very nice new clothes. We warned her that she was disobeying her spiritual authorities, and that there were important reasons for the guidelines.

Once again, she disobeyed and did the same thing. We ended up warning her a third time. However, a few days after the third warning, she called a leader in the church, and gave him the terrible news. That morning, her baby had drowned in his milk! The church had a funeral that day for her baby. God was trying to bring her into repentance, but it required Him to take some very severe measures to get her attention.

He Needs to Spend Three Years Under His Pastor

Many years ago, a young man felt the desire to work with us in the ministry. He was actually from another church, and the pastor of that church was helping him financially. He worked with us for a number of years and, in time, a serious weakness in his life was exposed over and over. I decided that he needed to return to his home church and submit to his pastor for three years.

At that point, he decided that he would not work any longer with us, and he made the decision to work with someone else. He did not want to return home for three years. From his perspective, everything seemed to be resolved by joining another ministry, but then he had a very serious accident and was severely injured. His pastor paid for him to return home, and it took him three years to recover from his injuries. He ended up submitting to his pastor for three years.

I have no doubt that, in this case, the Lord was showing him kindness, and was allowing his problems to bring a spirit of repentance to his life, and the victory over his weakness. What will your problems do—bring you closer to the Lord or cause you to harden your heart?

My hope is that the infallible proofs that have been shared in this book will cause you to see that there is a loving heavenly Father waiting to receive you and bless you. Ask Him to reveal Himself to you if you do not know Him, even if you have not believed that He exists! Ask Him to help you to repent of *your* ways and choose *His* ways. If you *do* know Him, then ask Him to reveal His care for you by showing you His infallible proofs that occur in your life in a new and greater way. May the Lord bless you!